The

SIMPLE

Method

for an Organized Life

Susan Walko

Cover design by Joanne Kenyon
Interior artwork by Madeleine Plaut; all rights with permission from Minuteman Press Lowell.

Library of Congress Cataloging-in-Publication Data is available.
Walko, Susan E.
The SIMPLE Method for an Organized Life

ISBN Print: 978-1-7354439-0-4

1. Organizing
2. Self Help
3. Life Skills

A heartfelt **_Thank You_** to everyone who has supported me in this endeavor

from its inception in 2005

to its completion in 2020.

And to you the reader,

for choosing this from the myriad of self-help, living your best life books.

Table of Contents

Chapter 1: Introduction

As a teenager, I babysat a family whose house was spotless and routines were not to be broken by adults or children, even when there was a babysitter. I remember thinking how unnecessary a routine it was for this family to soak their combs and hairbrushes once a week. Now I realize the importance that simple act of caring for their possessions played in the balance of the family's home life. The timeless adage this family lived by is something we should all strive for. If a person has too many possessions, they cannot care for those possessions in the way they deserve.

I used to think I would not be content until I had purged all the non-necessities from my existence. For a long time, my efforts to live a simple life with few possessions were unsuccessful. Each time I downsized my belongings, new items for which I was responsible magically appeared in my custody. I spent countless hours re-categorizing my stuff so it was more manageable. I made lists of the bare minimum possessions with hopes that having less stuff would make me less stressed. What were the extras that were causing stress? Books, movies, extra linens, board games, extra clothing, shoes, decorations, paper, craft supplies, extra household gadgets? The list went on and on. And so began my pursuit of living an organized life.

In exploring this topic, it became apparent my quest for organization was not just about things; it was about organizing *life*. My quest for organization was about not scheduling days so tightly that eating on the run was normal and drinking water was forgotten. My quest for organization was less about living without things, maintaining a perfect schedule, or organizing my kitchen. My quest for organization was about being mindful of my daily routines so I could continue to be healthy in mind, body, and spirit. My quest for organization was about simplifying my life so there was time to appreciate not only the important things but also the important people, in my life.

Let's start this journey by exploring a big-picture or macro view of the state of organization within ourselves and our culture. From an individual's point of view, organization is a cycle ending in stress. Stress occurs when you do not have control over a situation, and you think you can control it. It is worrying about what might happen.

The cycle begins with you living a peaceful life as an infant and then life circumstances happen. You need to earn money to survive, so you get a job. After a while, routine kicks in and you find yourself a little free time. So you begin a new venture and become, once again, strapped for time. You search harder for ways to cram the infinite number of things you feel obligated to do into a finite, inflexible amount of time. To help you do so, you reach for tools that promise to let you cram more things into less time. But things continue to get out of hand. You now have even more time, so you decide to make a difference in the world. You get involved in community activities, work more to increase your profits, or jump on the latest fitness craze to relieve the stress you're feeling from doing too much. The cycle continues until you eventually become even more stressed. The additional activity which may have begun to relieve stress creates even more pressure since now you have less unstructured time. This results in the inability to enjoy what should have been leisure time. You get stuck in a never-ending cycle.

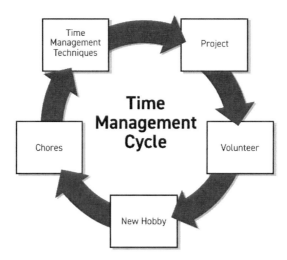

From a cultural viewpoint, we live in a disposable society. Even if you purge your own belongings and start living with the bare minimum like our caveman ancestors, what would that do? Other people around you would still be overconsuming. How many people would it take to go back to basics so there is no demand for the supply? Also, we are a people rushing from one thought to another without taking the time to process the inputs.

Do you never seem to have enough time to process all the inputs that are thrown at you daily? Do you feel like your brain is on overdrive so much that you have trouble sleeping? Or are you sometimes at your limit and just doing what is in front of you, even though you have not completed the already started and previously incomplete tasks? Is everything piling up?

**Sigh. **

We humans have created items and technologies to save time. We have even coined the term "multi-tasking" to describe our level of accomplishment in this realm. Many people brag about how many things they can get done at once. Woo hoo!

Just by pure advancements in technology, the tempo of life has increased over the years. As a society, we have increased our ability to access information while decreasing our knowledge of how to live.

By doing so, we have accelerated the pace of life to a point that we have forgotten how to enjoy life's simple pleasures. For example, consider seedless watermelon. Nowadays, you have a hard time finding good old fashioned watermelon with seeds. Because it represented extra work to remove watermelon seeds when you sat down to eat it, scientists have engineered watermelon without seeds. This saves time when eating. However, that saved time comes at a cost: taste. Many people agree that seedless watermelon is bland and dry compared to traditional, seeded watermelon.

What does watermelon have to do with organizing? It reminds us that life was not always this hectic. Humans originally lived by body time. The sunlight and the seasons ruled our lives. We used to eat when we were hungry and sleep when we were tired, not when it was clock time to perform these tasks. Now, here we are in the information age, too busy to read this book and too tired to care. Survival has become more complex and life has become a run-on sentence. We are a stressed society.

There is a better answer than eating seedless watermelon. Simplify your life so you can have time to enjoy the seeds.

This book will give you new tools to simplify your life without adding new stuff: possessions, work, or obligations that will simply re-clutter it. It will also show you how to use familiar tools in new ways. By using the tools and techniques in this book, even the ones you already know in different ways, you can simplify your life. The new tools this book introduces will enhance your humanity, not enslave you. You will learn how to process the information thrown at you so you can digest it in feasible sizes, keep what is important to you, and toss the rest away. After completing this workbook you will no longer need to "manage" everyday living. You will simply *live*.

Learning to simply live takes time and dedication. You will need to apply both as you go through this book. If you are the type that waits until the last minute to study for tests, prepare for meetings, and catch appointments, and you want to learn to simplify your life, before you dive in, stop and think. This workbook represents a big commitment. Yet odds are, if you picked up this book, you know something in the way you organize your life needs to change and you are ready to make that commitment. Stop now, take a breath, and agree to hold yourself accountable for the change you are about to make. If you don't, you will end up like the yoga student who always goes to the class but packs up before the final Savasana: neither relaxed nor enlightened, just sore from all that stretching.

When you come to an activity, I recommend finishing the entire activity, even if you have to set it down and pick it up a few times, before moving on. Take time to reflect on your current habits, decide if you want to change them, and then decide on the best way to do so.

How to Use This Book

Each chapter of this book introduces a new step in your journey towards simplifying your life and going from macro to micro. Within each chapter are strategies, tools, tactics, rules, and activities. I also include tips on how to effectively use the technology in your life under the topic "Electronic Considerations." Please note that electronic considerations are written without bias towards one particular technology or electronic platform so that it will be more easily translated to your preferred product. You also have a choice: you can skip to the "Quick Hits" section for actions that can be taken immediately or "Take it Deeper" by taking additional steps to attain the goals of the chapter. The symbols in the key below will guide you to the relevant sections of this workbook.

Key to the Symbols in This Workbook

Symbol	Concept	Meaning
	Strategy	A major step involved in achieving the goal of SIMPLE Organization
	Tactic	A specific way to achieve the strategy
	Taking it Deeper	Additional steps you can take to attain SIMPLE Balance
	Quick Hits	Quick actions that can be taken immediately to help you embrace the strategy
	Tool or Activity	A worksheet, exercise, or tool you can use to integrate SIMPLE Strategies into your life
	Rules	Reminders to your mind about answers to certain questions or routines.
	Electronic Considerations	Processes that can be performed electronically to achieve SIMPLE Organization

As I have said repeatedly, this is a workbook. Feel free to write down your answers to each activity on the pages, highlight the parts you find most relevant to you, and even scribble notes in the margins.

🕸 S.I.M.P.L. E – The Goal and Strategies

SIMPLE was chosen to remember to simplify. As I began thinking about my life as an adult, I kept thinking that "adulting" is much more complex than I imagined it would be. When my teenaged son said to me "Mom, you teach people how to be an adult," it hit me that my life-long journey of simplification has really about helping others learn from my journey. Now midway through my life, I feel I am officially an adult who is qualified to help others with obtaining a simple method of "adulting."

This section includes goal setting which is not only an important skill taught in classic time management classes, but also is crucial in organizing our lives. Goal setting is crucial as we learn to wade through the clutter of the mind and focus on the important.

This chapter focuses on the basics or simplicities of living: eating, sleeping, and breathing.

The primary goal throughout the book will be to simplify your life and the key strategies to achieve this goal are S.I.M.P.L.E.

Slow down

Introspection

Myself

Present

Lighten your load

Equilibrium

Slow down.

When we have so much to do to fulfill our basic needs, we tend to rush through our tasks. We try to cram "fun" into limited time slots. If you slow down, you will actually have more time to enjoy life, because you and will be focused on completing the tasks that matter the most. The main concept is containing all the distracting clutter that adds to life's chaotic pace in a way that puts it out of sight, but not out of mind. You will learn to create a place and system for holding items or papers related to tasks that need to be completed.

Introspection.

Introspection means to reflect inward toward yourself. To achieve any meaningful life change, you need to take the time for self-reflection.

Myself.

In this chapter, you will learn strategies to put your most important personal tasks first. Together, we'll examine how you spend your time and look at scheduling. I also include a lesson on which types of calendars work best in different situations: work, school, family scheduling, etc. and how to use a calendar effectively.

Present.

Living in the present means actually living, not just going through the motions, constantly reminiscing about the good old days, or dreaming of the future without taking action to achieve it. The strategy of being present concludes the time aspect of living a SIMPLE life. It ties all the other strategies together by showing you how to use a task list with the task drawer created in the Slow Down section. You will also learn how to prioritize tasks in conjunction with what is on the calendar you set up in the MYSELF section.

By the time you have completed these strategies, you will be halfway through your journey without even having picked up a single personal belonging or tossed out a strip of paper. That is because this workbook teaches you how to sustain your organization, and not fall into the trap of a single period of "getting organized." It discourages the one-time setting up a "pretty home" without putting systems in place to sustain it. The previous chapters have presented the structure. Now, you get into the actual picking up items and making decisions about them.

Lighten your load.

This section deals primarily with space. Decrease the number of basic things you need for survival. Decrease the amount of information you allow to be or actively put into your head. Learn how to find the things you need when you need them. The exercises in this chapter will help you see where their problem areas lie. Once you identify personal hot spots, you can use the tools you have learned in the earlier sections of this book to create a plan that will truly lighten your loads forever.

It is my view that you don't need to have a magazine, pristine photo home to be organized so this book is not going to show you the nitty-gritty of how to have a sterile-looking or immaculately organized home. Nor will it suggest the best or most fashionable containers for storage. This book will show you the process of organizing.

Since information is such a large problem in today's society, I have included an additional chapter on both lightening the load of both paper and digital information. That chapter can be summed up like this: Ignore the inputs available and trust in the information within yourself.

Equilibrium.

In all things, there must be balance. Even too much simplification is not healthy. The only way to stay on track is to consistently monitor progress and adjust where needed. The Equilibrium chapter of this book offers techniques you can use to remain balanced and stay on track with your newly learned healthy routines. This discusses putting routines on autopilot and creating systems so you can spend your time on the things that matter most.

One More Acronym- S.P.O.T.

In my line of business as a professional organizer, I help people through various stages of the process of organizing many facets of their lives. The tag line for my business is "Organizing Office, Home, and Life." If you are looking for office or home organizing, you simply need to refer to the *Lighten Your Load* chapters. However, in this book, as the title suggests, I am referring to LIFE organizing. This acronym, S.P.O.T., is what I use for clients who need total life organization. SPOT stands for:

Stabilize, **P**rioritize, **O**rganize, and **T**ransition.

You may be wondering why there are only four phases here, yet there are seven steps in the SIMPLE Method for an Organized Life. This is because SIMPLE is more comprehensive to include steps that only YOU can achieve without the intervention of another person.

Stabilize

The **stabilize** phase covers the strategies "slow down" and "get introspective." You need to root yourself before taking any steps, just like in the Tai Chi walk. For those of you not familiar with Tai Chi, the walk is the first concept learned. It teaches you to gently place your foot on the ground and get a firm feel for the surface before shifting your weight. This allows you to gracefully flow from one position to the other. During this phase, don't take on new tasks or responsibilities so you have the time to begin the macro planning.

Prioritize

During the **prioritize** phase, you continue the macro planning, which is the planning needed to achieve micro organizing. I give you the tools but you have to journey through the strategies: "put myself first" and "live in the present" in order to be successful and ready to move on to the "organize" phase.

Organize

Organize introduces the concept of zone organizing in which you learn to create specific areas for the various items that you own as well as designating spaces to accomplish your routine tasks. During the organizing process, you will evaluate the items needed so this phase also includes the "Lighten your Load strategy."

Transition

Finally, **transition** is the phase used when my client has or is ready to "attain equilibrium." Ultimately, I work myself out of a job because they are ready to embrace their new strategies. They are ready to remain organized for life. The *Attain Equilibrium* chapter will walk you through some of the techniques used to continually evaluate success and readjust as needed.

⌂ Rules of engagement for investing your time into this book

Rule setting is one successful technique used for creating a peaceful environment. Writing rules down further solidifies the ability to abide by them. One day, my children had a friend over and they were all hanging around the kitchen table. One of my children chastised the friend for not following the house rules. To his defense, he said, "I don't know the rules." So another of my children proceeded to bring out the rule book and review the house rules with the friend. We all got a good laugh at some of the rules, like "no wearing tap shoes in the kitchen" but it was apparent that having written rules is successful. They all knew what I expected, and I didn't even need to say a word.

Many people say that I am too rule-focused. One can't possibly follow all those rules. My answer is always the same: it is actually more freeing to put some rules into place. By having rules, your mind knows the answer to certain questions or routines so it can be free to think about other things.

Although rules will be discussed further in the *Attain Equilibrium* section, it will behoove us now to begin listing guidelines to follow when reading this book.

⌂ Read the book in order.

Although you technically do not have to read the book in chapter order it should be read in order to be more effective. Each strategy stands on its own. However, if you read them in order you will begin to understand that simplifying is a process as well as a goal and a strategy.

⬆ Spend the time to put the tools into practice.

To be successful, you need to give it time. It has been proven that to change your habits you need to commit to the new ones and work each day at them. Do not plan less than one week for reading each chapter. You need time to complete the activities and let the concepts sink in. When people get to point of calling an organizer (or reading a book) they already have a lifetime of "un-organization." The process will take time to transition to a new way of life. You need a commitment to your journey.

⬆ Only organize yourself and your personal space.

If you live with a person who is not ready for change you will need to work on yourself first and then you can begin to gain control over the shared spaces. The *Attain Equilibrium* chapter will address some guidelines for shared spaces.

⬆ Take small steps.

If you want success, you must be willing to step out of your comfort zone and try new things.

Finally, as with all good journeys, the last step is only the beginning of the next one. Hopefully, by that time, you are done with the book and you will be on your way to transition to a more balanced life of equilibrium and you can begin the life-long journey of micro organizing.

Thank you in advance for your time. I know it is precious. I hope that you will read each chapter with as much attention as I have given it. After all, your learning is my reward.

Chapter 2: 🕸 Simplify your Life

Life is a constant struggle to find ways to easily fulfill one's primary needs such as breathing, eating, and sleeping. Since we are born with the innate knowledge of these physiological functions, it should be simple, right? It isn't. However, the quality of life that we choose as adults is what complicates fulfilling our needs. We humans are frequently born into or stumble upon situations where our basic instincts are challenged and, as we proceed through life, we make poor choices that lead to a haphazard lifestyle. When we feel the need to manage our time, become more organized, or even get to the point of hiring a professional organizer, we may still struggle with the choices necessary to satisfy these basic needs. In other words, we are having trouble cutting through the muck and mire to make clear decisions.

Think about a spider who has woven a web with a purpose of gathering food. Up until this point, you have woven a web of your life, which most likely was done without thought and therefore may not have an apparent pattern or purpose. My job is to help you see clearly so you can make decisions that will delicately un-weave the web so it only contains items, people, and activities that support your purpose.

If you are like many of the people I work with, you may be thinking, "What is she talking about? I can make decisions." It is not uncommon that one might be able to choose alternatives for some situations but may struggle with putting those decision-making skills into practice in other instances. Or they may get distracted or tired. They may forget to or are too tired to follow through on decisions they have previously made. It is so often that people resolve to get organized but don't take the time to put away their belongings. In other words, they forget to act upon their choices and decisions.

Before we examine your choices and decisions making skills, read the Fisherman story, which illustrates how simpler choices can lead to a better quality of life.

The Mexican Fisherman

A businessman, on holiday, watched a little fishing boat dock at the quayside. Noting the quality of the fish, the businessman asked the fisherman how long it had taken to catch them.

"Not very long," answered the fisherman.

"Then, why didn't you stay out longer and catch more?" asked the businessman.

The fisherman explained that his small catch was sufficient to meet his needs and those of his family.

The businessman asked, "But what do you do with the rest of your time?"

"I sleep late, fish a little, play with my children, and have an afternoon's rest under a coconut tree. In the evenings, I go into the community hall to see my friends, have a few beers, play the drums, and sing a few songs. I have a full and happy life," replied the fisherman.

The man ventured, "I have an MBA and I can help you ... You should start by fishing longer every day. You can then sell the extra fish you catch. With the extra revenue, you can buy a bigger boat. With the extra money, the larger boat will bring, you can buy a second one and a third one and so on until you have a large fleet. Instead of selling your fish to a middleman, you can negotiate directly with the processing plants and maybe even open your own plant. You can then leave this little village and move to a city here or maybe even in another country, from where you can direct your huge enterprise."

"How long would that take" asked the fisherman?

"Oh, ten, maybe twenty years," replied the businessman.

"And after that?" asked the fisherman.

"After that? That's when it gets really interesting," answered the businessman, laughing.

"When your business gets really big, you can start selling shares in your company and make millions!"

"Millions? Really? And after that?" pressed the fisherman.

"After that, you'll be able to retire, move out to a small village by the sea, sleep in late every day, spend time with your family, go fishing, take afternoon naps under a coconut tree, and spend relaxing evenings having drinks with friends."

"And that is what I am doing right now," said the fisherman and went his way.

Adapted from short story by Heinrich Boll

(Boll, 1963)

After reading the Fisherman story, you may want to simplify your life and go back to nature, like the fisherman. But presumably, you are already in a situation which makes that unrealistic. However, you can make some small changes that will give you a sense of calm achieved by the fisherman.

Don't worry if your purpose is not as clear as the spider's web. As you begin to unweave the tangles, you may uncover something about yourself. And if you don't, keep plugging along. Life is about the journey, not only about the goal or "end game." And this book will take you through a journey of simple organization for life lasting results.

As people get older, they claim that they are out of energy to accomplish the things they set out to do when they were younger. They got sidetracked by life. Now they are too tired. So, I suggest, instead of giving up on those, get "un-tired."

The "Rat Race" now includes the technological drudgery that people get sucked into. They go to work by driving or taking the train. They use computers in their day to day life. They get home and use electronic devices to get food on the table just so they have time to "relax" in front of a computer screen or television. It's the same thing every day.

Like the businessman in the fisherman story, many of these people are serious about their careers, intent on fitting in with the neighbors, and always worried about doing the right thing. Others are just plodding along towards a day when they can finally rest. I am sure there as many other scenarios as there are individuals. But I hope my point is clear. People live life on a never-ending treadmill until they crash.

I do not think it is realistic to unplug totally from the technological world. A person living in an industrialized society is forced to purchase items such as food and vehicle fuel and therefore, cannot escape the clutches of industrialism. However, there is a chance to get un-tired and become an individual who is vibrant and has the energy of a child.

If you have not had the opportunity to live and un-tired life like the fisherman or do not remember that way of life from your childhood, let me give you a glimpse of what life can be like. You wake up naturally when the sun rises because you went to sleep when the sun set. You did not stay up late the previous night. When you wake up, you are greeted by your loving family. No one is grumpy without their morning coffee. You cut your locally grown vegetables with your favorite knife. You all go about the next few hours at a leisurely pace preparing for the day. Then you go about your daily tasks. Eat when you are hungry. Rest when you begin to feel fatigued. You greet every living creature with gratitude for being in your path that day and for the lesson they provided.

Do you like the scenario?

You do not have to wait until you are retired to get it. But you do have to make conscious choices about how you utilize your energy. By deliberately choosing your actions, you will naturally be less tired. As you re-group on your lifestyle, the decisions on what to accomplish in a day will begin to be about food and other healthy lifestyle choices. Days will be focused on loving acts to your family and friends. I suspect your shift will focus so that each day will be filled with compassionate actions towards all people and animals that cross your path.

So, to start you on this path, the next section in this chapter will help you focus your attention on learning to nurture your body and mind. How does this apply to organizing? If you are not able to think and act clearly, life will be a constant struggle of being unfocused and trying to get organized.

Please note as you read this chapter, that the suggestions presented are not medical advice. Before making any changes to routines that affect your health, consult with your physician and/or specialist.

Primary Needs

✂ Tool: Your Body

When starting to read a book on organizing your life, did you realize that health would be a key to achieving what you want in life? Your body is your best tool. You have it with you throughout your whole life. If you do not take care of your body, it will cease to function the way you want it to, and possibly even the way you need it to survive.

Make a pact with yourself not to beat on your body. What you really deserve is to have a body that can handle any situation with which it is faced. In addition to the standard recommendation of 30 minutes of exercise five times a week, you will need to do things like go to bed early, maintain a low stress level, and eat foods that do not aggravate your body.

Putting that into an easy list, there are only a few basic tactics to remember to keep your body functioning at an optimal level.

- ✓ Breathe deeply.
- ✓ Eat properly.
- ✓ Exercise daily.
- ✓ Sleep well.

You may need to re-learn these simple skills. They probably came easily when you were a child, but now you may have forgotten you need them to survive, perhaps because of the over-complications adult life brings. However, never fear. I have given you some tools and activities to help you re-learn these skills.

📌 Tactic: <u>Breathe</u>

You may think that you can cross breathing right off of your "task list" because this is something you do every day automatically. Why make it a chore? The truth is sometimes we neglect breathing deeply, filling our lungs with oxygen, because we are too busy running around to get everything on our "task list" done.

Breathing is the number one process that keeps you alive. Humans can last only about three minutes without breathing. How often do you really have to think about breathing? It should come naturally. But sometimes people forget their preferences for life: to breathe clean air and have healthy lungs. The following list will remind you that whenever you optimize your breathing you guarantee a calmer life.

- If you smoke, quit. Stop being around people who smoke. It is not easy. Please see your doctor or other health agencies for guidance and assistance.
- Be conscious of the quality of the air around you at home, work, and in the car.
- Practice meditative breathing regularly by starting with the "Clear the Clutter in Your Mind" Exercise.

✂ Activity: Clear the Clutter in Your Mind Exercise

Whenever you begin to feel that you are running on fumes or breathing shallowly due to stress try the **Clear the Clutter in Your Mind Exercise.** It will help you remember that breathing is life. You will need to find a quiet corner of the room or house during a time that will have no interruptions.

Sit on the floor with your legs crossed comfortably in front of you.
Close your eyes and concentrate on your breathing.

Listen to the air as it goes into your body and then back out.
Breathe in.
Breathe out.

As you breathe out imagine pushing the air to the spot where the tension has
        accumulated.
Relax your shoulders.
Relax your back.
Relax your legs.
Relax your toes.

As you breathe out push the air to each of your toes. Imagine all of the tensions going
        out of your body through your toes.

Relax your arms.
Relax your hands.
Relax your fingers.
Relax your head.

Tuck your chin in slightly so you can relax your neck muscles.

Imagine you are a marionette and the master has a string in the middle of your head and has just let your body go limp.

Totally relax your body. Concentrate on your breathing.
Breathe in.
Breathe out.
Feel the breath as it hits each of those relaxed muscles.

Slowly open your eyes.
Slowly breathing, begin to wiggle your fingers.
Continue the movement up your arms.

Wiggle your shoulders.
Roll your head.
Wiggle your toes and then your feet.

Continue the movement up to your legs.

Bend over as if you were bowing the floor. Stay like that as long as you need to collect your thoughts

✂ Activity: <u>Moving Meditation Exercise</u>

If you found "Clear the Clutter in Your Mind" Exercise too difficult because you cannot sit still for a long period of time, then try the **Moving Meditation Exercise.** Eventually, your mind will be calmer and you should be able to sit quietly and complete the Clear the Clutter in Your Mind Exercise.

Find a quiet corner of the room or house

Stand up with your feet slightly wider than hip-width apart and your arms at your sides. Slightly bend your knees.

Close your eyes and concentrate on your breathing.

Listen to the air as it goes into your body and then back out.
Breathe in.
Breathe out.

As you take in your next breath, lift your arms to the side of your body with palms facing up so that they are arms are parallel with the floor.

As you breathe out, move your arms above your head with palms facing together.
Breathe in.
Breathe out.

Turn your palms facing away from each other. As you breathe out, lower your arms back
    to your sides.

Continue this process for one minute. Eventually, work up to 10 minutes.

As you are lifting and lowering your arms and breathing, concentrate only on the
    movements of your breath and arms.

Imagine all of the tension leaving the body through your fingertips with each exhale.

My Tai Chi teacher would not be happy if I did not mention that this type of moving meditation can be an alternative to sitting meditation and has many additional benefits. To get into more depth about this topic, take a class on Qigong at your local martial arts studio or find a meditation class at your local yoga studio.

Tactic: Eat

Another essential life ingredient to be considered in keeping you grounded and prepared for the organizing journey is eating. You may be cheering, "Wow! Eating! Cool. I love eating as an item on my task list. I can eat better than anyone."

However, I challenge you to think about how what you eat or don't eat affects not only your body but also your mood. Have you ever been so obsessed that a cookie or piece of cake is waiting for you in the kitchen that you cannot even think about the work that you are supposed to be doing? Or have you ever been so hungry, that you couldn't finish a project? By being conscious of your eating, you will not only be combatting these types of woes, but you can also begin to see why having a handle on this simplicity of life will help you on your journey from macro to micro.

Eating is one of the most common obsessions in America today as evidenced by a large number of diet centers, weight-watching books, and food shows. Americans are obsessed with food. There is study after study on the causes of obesity and numerous counts of eating disorders such as anorexia and bulimia.

People eat for many reasons and at many different times. For example, people eat to calm their nerves, to take away boredom, because it is time to eat, or because food is available now and it might not be there later. To satisfy hunger and to gather strength are often low on the list of reasons why people eat.

Also, most people eat foods they like or want without giving much thought to the effect it will have on their bodies. They say things like "I deserve this piece of chocolate cake" or "This third helping of turkey with gravy sure tastes good" or "Let's see how much beer I can guzzle." You are what you eat! This old saying is very true. If you eat lots of greasy, high sodium foods, you will be a walking French fry. If you eat only low sodium, low fat foods, you will be a walking twig. Just as in all things, there needs to be a balance.

Eating begins with gathering, farming, gardening, and shopping. Then it includes washing, preparing, chopping, and cooking. Of course, when planning for our meals, we cannot forget the time to clean up after eating. In modern society, these are the factors that begin to complicate this basic need: packaging, shipping, preserving, adding chemicals, canning, and storage. We bring this upon ourselves because we expect to eat strawberries in winter or macadamia nuts from Hawaii although we do not live there. We also want preparation and clean up to be fast and easy, so we buy foods that can be easily thrown into the microwave or grabbed at a fast-food restaurant.

The simple task of nourishment has become big business. The choices these days are no longer simple. We have to choose between low fat, low salt, low sugar, low calories, and low taste. We have to watch the pesticides on vegetables, the hormones put in cows that end up in the milk we drink, the chemicals in boxed mixes, and many other things. No wonder the diet and fitness industry has kept up with the food industry. People need experts to tell them what, when, and how to eat.

When eating, think simple. Actually, when eating, think. Thinking when eating begins with knowing your body and what things are good and bad for it. Do not just throw something in your mouth because it is there. Think about your stomach and energy level. Are you really hungry? Or are you eating that donut because someone brought it in and you did not want to say, "no thank you?"

Think about what you are eating. Do not eat a lot of junk, or processed foods. For example, although there are more fats in a handful of peanuts than other snacks such as cheese doodles, the nuts may be the better option. It is interesting to watch children eat. They only eat junk food because their parents or television ads have taught them that way. When my children were babies, if they had a choice between plain spaghetti noodles with cheese on the side or lasagna loaded with cheese, they would choose the plain and simple spaghetti.

Plan what you are going to eat and you will be more likely to eat the foods that are good for you. Foods that are good for you do not have to taste bland or boring. This section will not attempt to teach you how to cook or tell what the right foods are to eat. However, with a little creativity and knowledge about simple eating principles, you can make anything to your liking.

I have spent years studying different theories about what constitutes a healthy diet. Here are a few concepts to help formulate new tactics regarding eating.

There is a happy medium between eating too much and too little or eating too much rich food and not enough calories. There are a few immediate rules about actions that you can follow to begin your never-ending process of eating for living.

⬆ Eat when hungry.

⬆ Eat to increase energy.

⬆ Eat a well-balanced, high variety menu.

There are many different theories on how much of what you should eat. The Food and Drug Administration's food pyramid says one thing, the macrobiotic theory says another, and the American Heart Association says something else. The list goes on. Basically, you should concentrate on eating a balance of carbohydrates, proteins, and fats.

Carbohydrates are basically sugar and come from vegetables, fruits, grains, and sweets. However, to stay healthy, the majority of carbohydrates should come from plants. If you are not a big vegetable person, you will have to work at finding vegetables that you like. Here are a few things to think about:

Vegetables should make up the bulk of the carbohydrate calories that you eat in a day. If you like a particular vegetable, ask yourself what it is that you like about it so you can try other vegetables with those qualities. Is it the sweet taste as in peas? Is it the bitter taste such as in Brussels sprouts? Or is it the smooth watery texture such as in cucumber? Do you like it better cooked or raw? Do you like the crunchiness of raw carrots or would you prefer them cooked?

Fruits, especially fruit juices, contain a large amount of sugar. You should limit the amount of fruit you ingest because large amounts of sugar will give you sugar highs followed by sugar lows.

Grain products are bread and cereals. Some diets such as paleo and keto tell you not to have any. Make sure if you follow any particular diet, you check with your health professional. There are many different ways to serve grains - cooked hot such as in oatmeal or rice, mixed with other ingredients, baked such as bread and muffins, or pan-fried such as pancakes and polenta. When eating grain products, it is important to keep in mind what percentage of the food is actually grain. A slice of cake with frosting is technically a grain but it is mostly refined and has a lot of added sugar.

Proteins can be plant or animal-based and provide essential amino acids or building blocks for the body. Animal-based proteins come from meat, poultry, fish, and dairy products. Animal-based products are complete proteins in one source.

Plant-based proteins come from legumes (bean proteins such as kidney and garbanzo beans) and nuts. Many vegetables are rich in protein. Some examples of these are broccoli, spinach, asparagus, and Brussels sprouts. Other vegetable-based proteins such as textured vegetable protein have been heavily processed. Vegetarian diets need to combine bean proteins with whole-grain carbohydrates each day to make up complete proteins. Being vegetarian requires a little more thought, but can be an alternative to diets high in animal protein. The key to selecting protein is to consider variety. When cooking, think simplicity.

Fats are an important part of a healthy diet. Fats fuel the body and help absorb some vitamins. They also insulate nervous system tissue in the body. Examples of edible animal fats are lard, fish oil, butter, and ghee. Examples of edible plant fats are peanut, canola, soybean, sunflower, and olive oils.

Fats are easy to distinguish in raw form but are often disguised in processed foods and animal-based proteins. Although a necessary part of our diet, if you eat too much of them, they add fat to your body. The typically recommended percentage of calories from fat is 30%. However, since many protein and carbohydrate sources already contain fat, the pyramid below shows 3% which represents the additional amount that you should really think about adding to your diet every day. In other words, adding butter to a sandwich may not be a wise choice since the bread and the items on the sandwich probably already contain enough fat for that meal.

In the below food pyramid, I have given the approximate percent of daily calorie intake that I have found helpful. My suggestions are only guidelines based upon researching the various food pyramids and simplifying to give people an easy way to keep track of what they eat without having a master's degree in nutrition. You can adjust these numbers based on your own needs. Your individual needs should be based upon the combination of elements that make up your original constitution. A doctor or licensed nutritional therapist can work with you specifically to determine the exact combination of carbohydrates, proteins, and fats you need, and even more specifically which carbohydrates, proteins, and fats are right for you. It is likely you will have to experiment with switching the amount of fruits and vegetables and the vegetables and grains. See how you feel having more of one and less of another.

For example, are you lightheaded because you had only fruit for breakfast and skipped lunch? Or have you realized that you cannot think straight only to realize that you did not eat enough meatballs but instead had extra pasta. Or maybe your stomach gurgles every time you eat pizza, but you love the taste of pizza so much you continue to eat it. The key here is eating for nourishing your body with simple foods and paying close attention to the feedback your body gives.

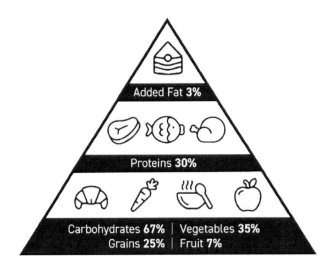

Broken down in a different way, to show the same information but gives you an understanding of what this translates to per serving.

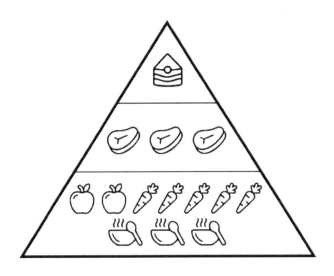

✂ **Tool: <u>Simple Eating Checklist</u>**

To put this healthy eating suggestion into everyday practice, use the **Simple Eating Checklist** to keep track of what you eat. This checklist is designed to help you stay disciplined on eating the proper balance of food servings each day.

Day	F	F	F /V	V	V	V	V	G	G	G	G	G /P	P	P	S	Extras
1																
2																
3																
4																
5																
6																
7																
8																
9																
10																
11																
12																
13																
14																
15																
16																
17																
18																
19																
20																
21																
22																
23																
24																
25																
26																
27																
28																
29																
30																
31																

On the chart, F= fruit, V= Vegetable, G = Grain, P= Protein, and S=Sweet. Below are some suggested serving sizes. They will vary for different body types and sizes as well as age. To find out how to adjust the average for yourself, please consult a certified nutritionist or doctor.

F= fruit	1 cup
V= Vegetable	1 cup cooked (2 cups raw leafy vegetables)
G = Grain	1/2 cup (cooked)
P= Protein	1/3 cup (cooked)
S=Sweet	1/2 cup

Although highly processed sweet treats and desserts are not really needed for proper body functioning, but they are a part of modern diets. As part of a simple eating plan, limit intake to one serving per day to allow your indulgence while curbing your binging. Sweets such as cakes and cookies should ideally not be eaten but if you do have them then count one serving as one grain AND the sweet serving. However, please do not forgo eating a healthier option so that you can have a piece of cake. It would be better to eat the sandwich contents without white bread and have two homemade whole-grain oatmeal cookies. For ascertaining an average serving size for sweets, check the label on packaged items or if homemade use the same as the predominant grain or protein in the item.

There is one column labeled "Extras" which is included to help record extra items that are eaten on days where you don't follow the plan strictly. It is a way to visually see how much extra food you are consuming. Ideally, this column should be left empty. As you are using the chart, notice at what times of the month or in what conditions you typically have entries in this column. If you are eating more than allotted on the chart, it could be that the chart is not right for your body or it could be that you are overeating. In either case, you should probably work with a professional to help you get on track with your simple eating tactics.

✂ Tactic: Exercise

Exercising is another important tactic in keeping your body healthy and ready for your journey. Keeping your muscles in good working order and your joints loosened should be automatic but we often lose sight of this basic necessity of life.

There are many theories about exercise. The common recommendations change daily. Should we exercise three times a week, five times a week, a half-hour each day, or two long workouts per week? Is it more important to do cardiovascular workouts or weight-training, or both? Were our ancestors concerned with this stuff? Did they take the time to weigh all of the theories then pick an exercise plan that was least hard on their schedule? Absolutely not. They were not worried about extra exercise because their lives were strenuous enough. In the technological age where everyone takes elevators up one level or drive across the street to the mailbox, people needed to develop exercise plans to recover the muscle mass lost during this inactivity.

There are a few general rules about exercise.

⬆ Exercise regularly.

⬆ Work movement into your day.

Exercise does not have to be boring and you do not have to go to the gym and pump iron to get exercise. Take a walk in the park. Walk upstairs instead of taking an elevator or escalator. Ride your bike two blocks to the bank instead of driving. When with children, play with them. Don't just sit back and watch them play. Clean out your basement. You can work up quite a sweat by lifting boxes of old things.

When exercising, think simplicity without a lot of complicated equipment and rules.

✂ Tactic: <u>Sleep</u>

Continuing on our exploration of the basic needs for our body to function well is sleep. Get adequate rest. It sounds easy, but the days of crashing anywhere to sleep are a few million years over. The standard in yesterday's world was to at least have shelter from nature's elements and, if you were lucky, a blanket to keep you warm. In today's society, sleeping becomes more complicated. You need to find a dwelling in which to reside. Within your residence, you will want a bed. These things cost money. To get money you need a job. For your job you need clothing. All of these choices just to provide for our simple sleep needs are

enough to drive you crazy and keep you up at night. Instead of staying up late and worrying about fulfilling these needs, sleep well.

There are a few initial steps that you can take to make sure that the sleep you get is restful. These should be added to the rules list so I have put the ⬆ rules icon in front of them.

⬆ Do not go to bed on a full stomach. Leave at least 2 hours before your last ingestion of food.

⬆ Create an environment that is inviting to sleep. No electronic devices in room. No clutter. Nothing under the bed period.

⬆ Keep a notebook and pencil on the nightstand to write down any thought that wakes you up. You will learn later in the book how to integrate these little notes into your daily life to accomplish tasks on them.

The items listed above are physical things that you can do to start you on a path to a restful night's sleep. I recognize that there are many sleep issues and disorders that are much more complicated than can be discussed in a book on life organization. If sleeplessness is something with which you struggle, please consult a sleep professional. Sleep is very important in keeping a clear mind.

✂ Tool: <u>Your Mind</u>

Your mind, next to your body, is the most important tool that you have. It controls your actions. It can reason. That means it has the ability to formulate ideas and learn from its mistakes. It also has willpower. It can determine cause and effect. And it has the ability to make choices and determine or predict the consequences of those choices.

How often do you really take care of your mind?

You are much more likely to react rationally to a situation if your mind is clear. If it is too clogged, it will turn to mush. Many people like to "vedge out," take breaks from their brain and pollute it with garbage, such as mindless television, drugs, or alcohol. Taking breaks is one thing, permanent vacation is another. Since you are reading this book you probably would like to improve this tool.

Once your mind is free of clutter and the exhaustion that comes from perpetual decision-making, you can expand and challenge your mind. You will have the mental capacity to take a course at the local college or an online class. Or if you cannot afford a class, select a topic to study and research it on your own. Anatomy and physiology might be challenging if you are an accountant. Computer programming might challenge you if you are a nurse. Drawing might bring out the creative side of an engineer.

Even if you choose to not study a new subject, do not close your mind. Use it to expand your horizons in other ways. Try reading something for fun. Even reading fiction teaches you how words go together, exposes you to new experiences or concepts you might otherwise not encounter, encourages visualization and imagination, and directly improves your reading AND writing skills. Audiobooks are a great substitute if you don't like to read, can't read for whatever reason, or don't have time.

✂ Tactic: <u>Clearing Your Mind Every Day</u>

Often when I am working with people on categorizing their spaces, they ask me how my mind can be so clear and focused when they easily get distracted. I used to say, practice your meditation but I have seen it happen many times. Practicing mindfulness and meditation in a controlled environment such as yoga studio is not enough to be able to translate this experience in everyday life. I wish I could say that there is an easy switch to flip, but there is not. It takes practice. Practice clearing the clutter in your mind at odd times and locations until you can do it without working at it. This will help you learn to integrate that technique into daily practice but to take it further you can't stop there.

Another way to achieve this is to cut out creating, or feeding off of, drama. Drama is energy drawing and it feeds the ego, but only temporarily so you need more of it to keep going. By cutting it out, you can again see clearly.

And finally, to really get the clarity you need, start evaluating your secondary needs and simplifying your life.

Secondary Needs

Now that you have humored me and read my dissertation about being healthy, you can now get on with the organization. Right? Nope! Now you have to do some thinking and planning. If you just want to start doing, skip to the "Lighten you Load" section. But let me warn you, physical action won't stick without internalization of concepts.

✂ **Activity: Personal Observation Questions**

Take some time to answer the questions below. This activity will act as a guide for what you want and will accept. It will help you see what is important in your life so that you can begin to make better choices about how you spend your time even on the basics of life, such as food, health, education, and love. Knowing and being consciously aware of the answers to these questions will help you make choices both on a daily basis and also automatically help you make choices about the basics of life. Feel free to expand your answers on separate pieces of paper if you need to.

- What do you genuinely enjoy doing?

- When do you feel like you are really "in the moment?"

- When have you felt like you would rather be somewhere else?

- Which people or group of people do you most enjoy being with?

- What have been your happiest moments? Why?

- If you had unlimited time and resources, what would you do?

- When you daydream, what do you see yourself doing?

- What are your important roles in life?

- What are some important lifetime desires you have in each role?

- What is your aim in life (career, family, other)?

✂ Activity: <u>Secondary Needs Worksheet</u>

Next, think about what are some of your secondary needs? For example, some important secondary needs are shelter and clothing. Their purpose is to protect you from the elements. Use the spaces below to describe the standards that you are willing to accept for these areas.

- Shelter (type, size, features, location, age, maintenance, shape)

- Clothing (amount, style, material, manufacturer/brands, and accessories):

- Transportation (type, model, quantity, age):

- Personal Belongings (grooming supplies, exercise items):

- Other (items for hobbies, memorabilia…):

Your list could probably go on for a long time. I will not talk *how* to fulfill ALL your secondary needs in this book. There are many magazines and books that can give you guidance on how to do that. However, to help you think about the tasks associated with fulfilling these needs, look at your list and ponder them in light of the following questions.

How often do you spend time maintaining the items on the list? Do you really need to do something so often? For example, do you really need to go out to eat once a week? Will it matter if you eat out once a month?

Do you really need to do something at all? For instance, if you do not need to wear clothes that require dry cleaning then you can eliminate a trip to the dry cleaners. Can someone else help you fulfill these needs? For example, is there a teenager in the neighborhood looking for a few extra dollars who wouldn't mind doing some yard work?

If you are genuinely interested in simplifying your life, then consider re-evaluating your secondary needs. The following section on goal setting will help you put structure to this re-evaluation.

✦ Tactic: Goal Setting/Action Planning

Getting caught up in the "busyness" of life and working harder and harder at climbing the ladder of success seems easy until upon reaching the top rung, you discover that the ladder is leaning against the wrong wall. This section addresses goals on a cursory level with hopes that your ladder will continually be not only leaning on the correct wall but also be centered in the proper spot. However, the intention of this book is to get down to the nitty-gritty of achieving goals.

It is helpful at this point to define various terms that are sometimes confused with the word "goal," such as the word "mission" or Mission Statement. A personal **mission statement** is a description of your life's purpose. It is a one to three sentence motto of how you envision living your life. Creating a personal mission statement helps you identify your values so you can keep your focus when making decisions and guides you when determining what goals are most important.

To understand your mission, think about the way you look at life. It is not a destination. It is a way of being. For example: Do you see everything in terms of money? Or do your actions revolve around having friends or helping people? Here is my mission statement as an example: "Respect the world around me, including people and things. Remain in the background so I can help people become their best version of themselves." Some other good examples are: "To inspire success through teaching," "To create the best version of tomorrow," and "To be kind to others and myself."

A **goal** is a desired future condition and is expressed in either quantitative or qualitative terms. A goal is usually driven by needs, wants, or desires. For example, you may have made the following statement: "I am always tired and listless." What you really mean is "I seem to be tired at work." Therefore, your goal would be driven by your need for more energy and would read "to be energetic and vibrant during work." Some other examples of goals: "Be more attentive to people in my life," "Focus on being more proactive instead of reactive," "Get out of debt," and "Finalize Divorce."

The critical part of goal setting is that the goal be written and not just in your head. Unless it is written, it is merely a dream or a wish. It is outside of reality.

Some people would argue that goals are not necessary. Why set yourself up to struggle to make your life meaningful and have purpose? However, I argue, if you do not set goals or have a mission, you end up "going with the flow." You may roll down the swiftly flowing river with no boat or paddle and sink like a stone or take a chance and go wherever the river wants to take you instead you leading yourself in the direction you are meant to go.

The concept of goal setting is natural. Without humans setting goals, the wheel and fire may not have been discovered. Goals are merely tools to guide us. They help us evaluate where we have been and where we are going.

Goals without a plan to execute them are overwhelming. So are unrealistic goals. Goals should be specific, achievable, and, in the case of life goals, the end result should be sustainable. The process of achieving the goal should enforce the habits necessary to sustain the goal on autopilot, without having to think about it.

In goal setting, we need to break the goal down into strategies. A **strategy** is a major step involved in achieving a goal and is directly related to the goal. A strategy has a shorter time frame and a narrower focus. For example, if your goal is to climb a mountain you may need several strategies such as building up stamina or increasing muscle strength or better breath control.

A **tactic** or action plan is a way to achieve the strategy. For example, if you have the strategy of lightening your load by having fewer belongings, one of the tactics may be to categorize the belongings that have piled up. You would then break up the tactic into manageable tasks.

Each **task** is the smallest unit needed to be done. The tasks equate to your "task" list. Each one is detailed and fully thought out and has a specific deadline for completion. It is also obvious as to if or when each task has or has not been accomplished. By assigning to yourself one little task per day, the goal will seem attainable. A task is a method of achieving your strategy and should not be considered a goal. To further break down the tactic of categorizing your belongings, one large category may consist of excess paper that needs purging. Some tasks may be:

- Gather all of the papers into one location

- Separate the piles into categories
- Sort pile from bedroom floor into keep and recycle
- Create a file folder to store papers from bedroom floor

Putting It All Into Action

Goal setting will help you determine what you **want** to do. Then you will address what you **need** to do in order to achieve it, and more importantly what steps you can take to actually complete it. In other words, you need to create a plan. Planning involves seeing ahead and determining what activities will need to be done to complete a project, goal, report, or assignment. By taking the time to plan, you start putting how you spend time into perspective.

A student of time management would learn that to plan will help one reach his or her goals. My view is much more simplistic. Planning will make you available for the opportunities that are thrown your way. It is easy to manage time when systems are small, and inputs are few. As daily inputs get more numerous, the course of your day begins to change rather quickly. Planning helps you navigate the river of life, so you are prepared for changes in the course of the day. It will allow you to handle them with the calmness of a Buddhist monk and still stay on the path that you are destined to be on.

As you invest more time in planning, you will naturally be doing the things that are personally valuable and not the ones that relate to simply putting out the fires of the day. You'll find that you spend far less time picking up the broken pieces or reacting to the urgent demands of others.

There are two types of planning, long-range and short-term. We address long-range planning when we look at goal setting. The time frame for short-term planning is generally anywhere between a day and a month.

Again, this book is more about goal *achieving* rather than setting. The concept of creating a vision for your life will be introduced in order to show the steps necessary to break them down into achievable tasks that have a chance of getting accomplished.

It is this short-term planning that many people have a hard time understanding. They often have a large project but don't have a plan for it. They get overwhelmed and give up. This section will show you how to focus on short-term planning. The first thing is to break it down into smaller tasks. For example, if I wanted to write a book, I may need to determine a topic, research it, write an outline, schedule time to write, and so on.

So, let's get started.

✂ Tool: <u>Pencil</u>

Get yourself a good mechanical pencil or a pencil and a good sharpener. Make sure to get a working eraser. On all of the activities, especially the task list and calendar, you will need to be able to erase and easily make changes.

✂ Activity Step One: <u>Writing a Mission Statement</u>

Use the answers from the Personal Observation Activity to help direct your thinking to write a mission statement. Your mission statement should be no more than three sentences to describe what is most important to you.

This will be helpful later to help determine the personal benefits gained by achieving one of your goals. You need to be able to articulate why the goal is important to you personally. And the mission statement will remind you of the why.

✂ Activity Step Two: <u>Take Your Pulse – Life Organization Needs Symptoms Worksheet</u>

Do your life organization skills need an adjustment? Look at your own lifestyle and think about the way you feel at the end of each day. Are you truly happy with the way you are utilizing your time? There are symptoms you can look for to see if you need to make some changes to your habits. Identifying these symptoms, then making a conscious effort to modify your behaviors can help you (and your family) live a happier, more productive life. Consider the statements below and check all that apply. Add other items as well that may indicate you need an overhaul.

☐ I don't feel healthy.

- ☐ I tend to eat erratically.
- ☐ I don't have time to spend with people.
- ☐ I have anxiety.
- ☐ I have no desire to do anything.
- ☐ I cannot sleep.
- ☐ I am always tired.
- ☐ I have no life - my life is all work.
- ☐ I am irritable often.
- ☐ I am depressed.
- ☐ I am a "rush-a-holic."
- ☐ I never smile anymore.
- ☐ _____
- ☐ _____
- ☐ _____

If you are like most people that exercise is not too easy. It is often easier to see the signs of stress in others than in yourself. The symptoms that you listed above are probably obvious. You can probably feel them. Anyone can see them. But why do you have them? You may have too much to do and not enough time to do it.

✂ Activity Step Three: <u>Set Your Goal</u>

Use the following steps to set goals and then list one goal that you want to accomplish in the next year.

1. Determine your goal. If you are having trouble coming up with goals, make a list of everything you have always wanted to do, be, or have. Ideas prompt more ideas, so let your imagination run wild. Sometimes you will think something is impossible, but add it to the list, anyway. It may be within reach if you set your mind to it. You can also look at your symptoms for ideas. Or you can use as an example your need to make a change to your time management habits.

2. Write your goal. Restate your symptoms positively and these will become your goals. Use action verbs and state your goal in the present tense as if it were a reality now. Be as specific with them as possible. This helps establish a finish line.

3. Add measurement methods. How will you know when your goal is accomplished? The more specific the goal, the easier it is to measure progress. For example, instead of writing "lose weight," write down the exact number of pounds you want to lose. If you want to "be vibrant and energetic at work," create concrete goals such as smiling at co-workers, or entering the work environment in a happy frame of mind. Is there a definite end? Usually, it will be a disappearing of the symptoms that caused you to write the goal. Again, write what you want the end result to be and phrase it in positive terms.

4. List the obstacles. Before you can begin to achieve your goals and strategies, you need to understand the barriers preventing you from achieving your goals. List people or other barriers that will make it harder for you to achieve your goal. Some obstacles might be:

   - I have a small child who is keeping me up at night.

   - I don't enjoy the work that I am doing.

   - The work I have is too hard.

   - I am always taking care of other people's requests before doing my "real" work.

   - I have too many things to do.

   - I am constantly losing time in meetings.

5. Next, put an estimated completion date on your goal. List a realistic time frame to complete it. Take into consideration your current responsibilities and when you might have to break off from the task or if there is a built-in deadline. For example, if your goal is to lose fifty pounds, one week is not a realistic time frame for completion. You will have setbacks to achieving your goals, but having clear strategies with time frames helps you stay on track better.

6. Check your goals against these questions:

   - Is it explicit?

- Is it a single goal?
- Can it be reached in the time frame you set?
- Can the achievement be measured?
- Has it been thought out fully?
- Does it have the correct outcome in mind?
- Is it really my goal or is it some other person's goal?
- Is it important to me?

Goal: _____

Measurement Methods:

_____

_____

_____

Obstacles: _____   _____

_____   _____

_____   _____

_____   _____

Estimated Completion Date: _____

Select no more than three goals at a time on which you would like to improve. Choosing more will not allow you to fully concentrate on any one effectively. Also, try to select goals that relate to different areas of your life (home, family, work, self, etc.) instead of concentrating all three within one area. This helps create the equilibrium in life you are looking for. Additionally, it is wise to choose different areas to avoid the imbalance that could be caused by a neglected area.

✂Activity Step Four: <u>Create Strategies</u>

Write strategies for each of your goals. Remember that multiple strategies help guide your choice of actions to accomplish the goal. Strategies are ways that you can achieve the goal. For example, for the goal is to live a simpler life some strategies might be: slow down, lighten your load, and so on. As another example, if your goal is to lose 40 pounds in a year then your strategies might be: plan daily food intake every Sunday and exercise at least an hour a day four days a week.

✂ Activity Step Five: <u>Create an Action Plan/ Begin Action Planning Worksheet</u>

This next step to create an action plan is most often overlooked, yet it is most important. The first part of creating an action plan is to break down the strategies into more manageable tactics. As there were several strategies per goal there should also be several tactics per strategy. To start planning your tactics, write down ways to achieve the strategy. If the goal is to lose weight and the strategy is to exercise more frequently some tactics might be: Go to the gym, Get more exercise in daily life, and go on outings which are based around exercise.

To take it to the next level and plan tasks, use the gym example. There is more than writing on a list "go to the gym." If you don't belong to a gym, you need to research gyms, test them out, make a decision, pay, get appropriate clothing, find out about times and classes, etc. This is where you begin to break the tactic into accomplishable tasks that can eventually be checked off a list.

You will use the Action Planning Worksheet to guide you through this process. This sheet can be used for many different purposes other than planning your strategies or tactics. It could be used for planning a project or it could be used for something as simple as planning a yard sale or a phone call to someone.

Action Planning Worksheet

Subject:	
Begin Date:	Due Date:
Information:	

Sequence	Action/Task	Start Date	Due Date	Notes

Start by writing a brief description of the strategy or tactic in the **Subject** section.

Next enter the **Due Date**. This is the date that you need to be totally done. Sometimes you do not have a due date. You may need to start with today and then back into a due date. Don't worry about it now if you have trouble filling in the date column. Hopefully, after reading the Living in the Present chapter, you will be better equipped at setting the due dates.

If there is additional information needed for this subject, list it in the **Information** section. Other information could be contact person, phone number, website URL, or notes about the subject. For example, if the action being planned was to get new window treatments, you might list the size and quantity of windows in the information section so when you are researching you have the information handy.

Next, make a list of tasks that you need to complete in the **Action/Task** column. For example, if your tactic was to have a yard sale some tasks might be: set date, gather items, advertise, get change, determine prices, and enlist helpers.

Many people get tripped up at this phase because they know that they can't currently think of all the steps. Therefore, they don't even start a project or listing actions to complete a strategy. That is ok. Use this sheet as a way to initially brainstorm as many tasks as you can think of during the initial planning session with yourself. You can always add tasks as you think of them. Sometimes if you know you are going to have a project but are not yet ready to start it, you can fill in the header information on the worksheet and add tasks as you think of them. Then, when you are ready you will have the tasks all listed.

Next, use the s**equence** column to rank your tasks in order. What has to be done first, second, and so on? Sometimes the order may change as items are completed and new items are added. Also, the logical order is not always the best answer. In the book example, I may want to find an agent before I finish the book but may need to wait until I have a concrete outline or sample chapter.

Finally, plan **dates** for accomplishing the actions. After you put the tasks in order, depending upon due date, you can work backward (or forwards) to figure out what date to do work on and complete each task. Often people miss this step and get to the due date of the entire project before they realize they should have started it long ago. Having a plan allows you to be prepared for unexpected circumstances that may arise. Writing it down allows you to be freed from the burdens of the whole project so you can focus on the current task. In Put Myself First, Prioritize and Live in the Present chapters you will learn to prioritize them and set estimated completion dates and eventually transfer them to a daily or weekly task list for completion.

Action Planning: Real-World Example

One client I had was very creative and always had many ideas flowing through her brain to the point where she would stay up a night thinking about them. She utilized the action planning sheets to help take all those ideas out of her mind and put them in a place where she could not only ease her mind but also set her up for accomplishing many of the ideas. To do this she created a binder with tabs for each letter of the alphabet. Then as she thought of projects, she could write the header for it and as ideas came up, it was easy to flip to the page and add more tasks. Finally, when she was ready for one tackling of these projects, she could prioritize the tasks and integrate them into her daily task list for completion.

The **notes** column is used to track additional information. For example, a task of call about dumpster pickup for a basement clean out project might include the phone number of the dumpster place.

One final word about setting action plans. After you associate dates with tasks, you should write the tasks on your daily task list so you won't forget to do them. You will be able to live in the present and when the time comes you will know that you have to do them. In the *Live in the Present* chapter, you will learn more about how to integrate the tasks from the Project Planning Worksheet. For now, use the **Action Planning Worksheet** to plan for completing one of your tactics and keep it with this book. To get copies of this worksheet for additional planning, please visit our website at www.organiz-er.com/publications.html.

⚲ Taking it Deeper

After setting the goals and learning about action planning, you will be no better off than where you started if you don't have discipline. To help you gain discipline, make yourself accountable. Ask a friend to check in on your progress. Also, remember that you do not have to accomplish it all in a day. Keep your eyes on the prize and that slow and steady wins the race.

⏲ Quick Hits

- Remember your basic primary needs are simple.
- Do not try to complicate a situation and create more needs than necessary.
- Schedule both primary and secondary need fulfillment as if they were equal.
- Honor your primary needs first. Just a reminder they are: breathe, eat, exercise, and sleep.
- When prioritizing your daily tasks, do not automatically shift primary needs to accommodate the secondary ones. In other words, don't sacrifice healthy eating so you can complete a goal such as building a gazebo.

Chapter 3: 🕸 Slow Down

If you are moving too fast, you cannot recognize opportunities because you will not see them. As I am editing this book, yet again, the world is experiencing a pandemic health crisis due to Coronavirus (COVID-19). The federal, state and local government officials are urging me, along with everyone else, to limit contact with others in hopes to minimize the virus' spread. The situation is naturally causing us all to slow down. How appropriate that this is the chapter I left off editing two months ago. I had gotten so busy servicing clients, that I did not take time to finish the final editing process.

Thank you, world, for reminding me to slow down.

Whether you are reading this book because you are the one who is going at five hundred miles per hour and trying to cram twenty-eight hours into a twenty-four hour day or life itself is going too fast or the world is going too fast for you, you can benefit from taking the time to ponder the ideas that will be presented in this chapter which are all dedicated to going S L O W E R.

Identify a time-saving device that you feel you cannot do without. Perhaps it is your weed whacker, dishwasher, microwave, or blow dryer. What would happen if you went without that device the next three times you needed it to perform your task? Would you complete the task on time? Would it take longer? Would the task be more enjoyable? Would it even be doable?

Now think about how these modern-day conveniences affect your life. For example, instead of using the snowblower this winter, you could try a shovel, assuming you are able-bodied and have no health issues? You will not have to deal with purchasing gas/oil mixture. Nor will you have to take the time to fill it. Nor will you have to worry about storing, cleaning and maintaining the snowblower. You will get exercise thus maybe eliminating a trip to the gym. Shoveling by hand for 60 minutes burns 527 calories. Walking behind a snow blower burns fewer calories and may take 30 minutes which burns 197 calories. As a bonus, you will have gotten sufficient vigorous exercise needed to balance blood sugar. Plus, shoveling by hand will be friendlier to the environment.

Here are some other questions to consider: Do you make more laundry because you have a washing machine? Do you take more trips to the grocery store because you have a car? Is it easier to get rid of a pair of pants with a missing button than to sew on the button? Your life may be easier in some respects, but is it better? If we slow down our minds and actions, we can begin to simplify our lives. Simplification will ultimately allow us to be better equipped to enjoy our lives.

Rushing all the time rubs off on others around you and causes stress for you as well as them. There is often no need for it. When I was pregnant, I initially tried rushing around to finish all of my open projects and tasks but at some point, I realized that I would not have the time for completion. So instead of trying to fit everything into my remaining days at the office, I started making a list of all the projects for work that I did not want to start until I returned from maternity leave. This list filled a whole page and I was worried that the bosses would not be happy because I could not complete the projects. As it turns out, the undue stress I caused myself and my fears were pointless. At the end of my two-month maternity leave, the need for these projects was no longer necessary because the entire company was re-structured, and the big boss in my department was eliminated. Company priorities had changed dramatically. In retrospect, it was a blessing that I did not waste my energy rushing to get those remaining projects and tasks done before I went on maternity leave.

One of the visible signs that we are in a society of rushing people can be seen every day when driving anywhere. People tend to cut in front of others so they can zoom by the car in front of them. It is getting more noticeable every year. People are now even impatient to slow down at a yellow light. Instead, they speed up and more often than naught blaze through red lights. When I was in driver's education, we saw an example of two people leaving a destination at the same time to get to the same place. One drove recklessly to get there as quickly as possible and the other drove at the speed limit and observed all road rules. In every test that was performed, the maximum time difference between the two cars was five minutes. Think about this. While in the car for those extra five minutes you can turn off the radio, drive with a stress-free attitude, and prepare for wherever you are going. When you get to your destination, you will be alive and prepared for living in the present. More importantly, you and your car will be intact.

What are the signs that you are in a rush? Are you always tapping your foot or constantly moving? Are you impatient when a child or elder takes longer to do anything? Did you wish you could skip any process and just move straight to the results? Do you get crazy when people ahead of you are driving too slowly? When you are working at your desk, do you find yourself trying to squeeze in "just one more thing" before standing up from your desk to go to the restroom or eat lunch?

✂ Activity: **Assessing Your Speed Tolerance**

Take some time to determine your style of achieving tasks by completing the **Assessing Your Speed Tolerance Exercise**. For each statement, circle the number that applies to you.

1	2	3	4	5
Always	Often	Sometimes	Seldom	Never

After a meal, I have to clear the table and wash the dishes immediately.	1 2 3 4 5
I go grocery shopping when the milk is ¾ gone as opposed to waiting until I only have the ingredients to make an onion sandwich.	1 2 3 4 5
I would rather wash laundry every day than wait until I have no clean underwear.	1 2 3 4 5
I need to have three packs of toilet paper in the house at all times and would become very anxious if we ran out and had to use tissues.	1 2 3 4 5
I make my bed every day as soon as I am out of it.	1 2 3 4 5
My paperwork is complete at the end of the day.	1 2 3 4 5
I cannot sleep at night because I keep thinking of all my tasks that are not finished.	1 2 3 4 5
My lawn has to be perfectly groomed. I cannot stand my grass when it is more than 2 inches long.	1 2 3 4 5

If you answered with mostly 1's and 2's, you will need to spend extra time on forcing yourself to slow down. Try this activity: force yourself to wait to do a regular chore. For instance, what if you chose not to do the dishes right away? Simply, pile them up and relax or play a game after a meal.

If you answered with, mostly 3's you are right on with balancing slow and busy times; however it is always good to check yourself to stay on track.

If you answered with mostly 4's and 5's, you already know how to slow down. You may want to look back at your answers to determine if you need speeding up. Sometimes being too slow is just as unhealthy as being too quick.

Whatever category you fit into on the speed tolerance questionnaire, it is very important to be aware of your mindset. Do you need to force yourself to slow down or are you too slow and need to speed up?

If you are already slow by nature, don't think you can get off easily and bypass this chapter. Many of my naturally slower-paced clients struggle with life organization. This chapter is as much about minimizing distractions than it is about slowing down. The letter "S" for Slow Down was chosen as a touchstone to remind you that learning something new takes time.

It is okay to thrive on chaos, but not at the expense of yourself and others. Sometimes by rushing around and not focusing, you miss out on the enjoyment of the task. If you are constantly putting out fires, then you will always be too busy to enjoy what you are doing, even if it's the process of putting out those fires. When you slow down, there is more time to savor the moments and spend time doing the things that matter.

When you have so much to do to fulfill your basic needs, you tend to rush through your tasks. You try to cram as much as possible into limited time slots, sandwiching tasks between the basic needs.

There is one hilarious episode of the sitcom, *I Love Lucy*, where Lucy and her best friend Ethel work at a candy factory. Their job is to wrap candy as it comes through a conveyor belt. At one point the manager comes over and sees what a great job they are doing at the rate candy is coming off the conveyor belt. The manager decides to turn up the speed of the conveyor belt so they now have to wrap more candy in the same amount of time. Faster and faster the belt flies until the audience sees Lucy and Ethel stuffing the candy down their shirts and in their mouths just to keep up with the amount of candy passing by them. (Jess Oppenheimer, 1952)

This episode is a great example of how people tend to handle paperwork and other inputs coming to them daily. They just keep stuffing it somewhere and more appears. They never get a chance to process all of the inputs because there are just too many and they don't take the time to make decisions about it right away. As you begin working with this SIMPLE organizing system, think of ways that you can decrease the number of inputs coming your way so you can slow down and handle them completely instead of finding ways to get them out of sight and out of mind until maybe someday you have the luxury of dealing with them.

To begin, you will need to learn patience. The saying goes: patience is a virtue. But how can you develop patience? Patience refers to waiting and listening to what the world has to offer. Instead of forcing the world to fit in your plans or control a situation, sit back and wait for the cues the world is sending.

You may be thinking, "Hey wait a minute! In the last chapter, you mentioned goal setting so we can steer our path and now you are saying don't force the world to fit in your plans." These two concepts may seem contrary to each other but they are not. There is an order to the universe. You just need to notice it. Once you do you will begin to have synergy with your plans and that of the universe.

In addition to having too many inputs that speed up our pace of life, we tend to create distracting clutter that adds to our chaotic pace. One way we create clutter is by leaving items and paper in view (in sight and mind) to remind ourselves what we have to do. We are afraid if we put something away we will forget about it. How can you get out of this spiraling maelstrom? The answer is to create a system to contain all incoming inputs so they can be processed and do not get out of hand. Now that you have an understanding of your style as well as a better appreciation of patience, you may have brain space to begin the SIMPLE funnel system that I have used for years to help me manage all the inputs presented to me.

📌 Tactic: The SIMPLE Funnel System

Think of a funnel used to control the flow of oil into a reservoir. The funnel is needed to squeeze in oil without leaking all over the other parts of the machine. Just as the funnel prevents spillover and possible fire hazards, you will be controlling items, paper, and tasks coming into your desk and home. In other words, you can slow down the pace of your inputs to match your tolerance.

In order to utilize the Funnel System, you will learn to funnel into one place all tasks that you need to accomplish. Whether it is a new pair of pants that needs to be integrated into your daily life or an invitation to a wedding, all items coming into your existence need your attention. This SIMPLE system starts with three physical tools:

1. **Inbox.** This is a space in which all inputs will be temporarily stored, including the pair of pants or the receipt from a larger item that may not fit into a box. This system explains how to set up a physical Inbox. Your e-mail Inbox may be another source of inputs and should be handled in the same manner as the physical Inbox. A note on a scrap paper in your physical inbox can remind you to process the new e-mails in the electronic inbox.

2. **Task logging tools.** The task list is a necessary item that individuals should use to help direct their efforts throughout the day. By listing the scheduled and unscheduled demands upon your time, you can save your brainpower for actually completing the commitments and hopefully have energy left over for leisure time activities.

3. **Task filing system.** At minimum, a task filing system consists of a task file box. Some additional tools are the "Work In Progress (WIP) Area" and the "Backlog Area." The entire system is a way to control the inputs that you receive so you can handle them when you are ready. One of the biggest issues I see when working with people on organizing is having a place to keep track of the paper and items required to complete a task. As part of this system, you need to commit to utilizing a task list (paper or

electronic) and designate an uncompleted task area in your home which will include a task file drawer or box.

Let's get started by gathering the supplies needed as well as designating the locations for storing items.

✂ Tool: **Inbox**

An inbox can be made of any material. The most common types are wooden or plastic boxes which can be obtained at any office supply store. The inbox should be approximately 9 inches wide by 13 inches long and should be no higher than three inches tall. If it is taller, there will be a tendency to not clear it out regularly.

The inbox should be placed in an area that is convenient for all members of the household. Usually, a kitchen or entryway is the best location. This will allow anyone to add papers or other items to the inbox. Being in a convenient location will also allow the inbox manager (you) to monitor how full it is. Later on in the book, you will learn about clearing the inbox. Right now create the inbox and put it in a convenient location.

✂ Tool: **Task List**

The task list is for activities that do not already have a time associated with them on the calendar. When I first started my career as a Time Management trainer and then later a Professional Organizer, I used to recommend a daily task list associated with the calendar. However, as time passed and I saw how people really utilized lists, I created a weekly task list. It takes some of the pressure off already busy people that constantly feel like they have to continue checking off completed tasks. In other words, it creates some breathing room for always being on the go, go, go. I use the following the **Weekly Task List** with many of my clients. It is a place to keep track of all of the non-routine activities you have to accomplish. Here are some examples on my current list for the week: select date for family summer gathering, create new worksheet to use with clients, call friend asking her if she wants something for her cats, and text son about a new recipe. You would not list items such as prepare lunch or get dressed on your task list because these are routines that typically have a time frame associated with them. If you do want a place to list these and other routine activities, you would enter them in your calendar. How to balance routines with non-routine task is addressed in the *Attain Equilibrium* Chapter.

Weekly Task List

Week of: _____

✓	Priority	Task

Remember to:

Notice also there is a call outbox labeled "remember." This is a place to write the one underlying thing you want to remember this week. Some items I have written there: get outside, practice playing triplets on my instrument, drink water, and sign son up for his class. Others have used it to remember a login ID or a recipe they want to remember. I just caution that it should not be something you want to remember past the current week because when a week is over, you will not go back to that page. Everything will be completed or transferred to a new week.

🖥 Electronic Considerations: Electronic Task List

If you are using an electronic task list, then you do not need a paper one. The only way for you to get a handle on the tasks you need to complete is to funnel them all to one place. If you sometimes need to write tasks on paper because you do not have your electronic system at hand, it will be necessary to transfer them onto the electronic list later.

If you are on the computer or other electronic device often, then I recommend using an electronic task list found as part of any good electronic calendar/organizing program. An integrated electronic system offers an advantage because it encompasses task, calendar, and e-mail. You can simply drag the e-mail to the task folder. If your e-mail system is not attached to your task list, you can cut and paste the information from the e-mail into the task list. However, if you do not have a computer or smart device or would prefer to use paper, the system is flexible and can be used with any method you choose.

Tool: <u>Task Drawer or Box</u>

A key part of accomplishing the tasks on your list is to determine what items are needed to complete them. Often people have items strewn all over the counter, desk, or house because they fear they will forget to do the task if the items are put away. The solution to controlling this clutter and/or chaos is to create a file folder or drawer that stores in one place any items needed to  finish tasks. It will be easier to find the items when you are ready to start work on the task.

To set up a Task Drawer you will first need an empty file box or drawer. If you are integrating a drawer, it should be the one located closest to your work surface or desk. This will allow easy access during the time you are working on the task. Using a file box is good because it is portable and can be used anywhere; however, unless you have a safe out-of-the-way place in which to store the file box, it can be unsightly.

Some consideration also needs to be given for the location of where you typically do tasks. If you normally are based in one location, then a task drawer will work well. If you are on the road often, you may need to adapt your area to a smaller, more portable device such as an accordion folder.

Real Life Example

One client came to me because she was overwhelmed and unorganized. Her husband had recently had a stroke and there was no way to keep track of the paperwork that was piling up. Since he had done most of the paperwork during their almost 50 years of marriage, she was hit with double the responsibility. During the initial assessment, I suggested that her only issue was that she was losing track of tasks that needed to be completed. In all other aspects of her life, she was organized and diligent about keeping a task list. She had a bunch of papers sprawled around her office, so she wouldn't lose track of them. Once we set up a Task Drawer, she no longer felt like she was spinning out of control.

Once you have decided which type of file container you are going to use, the second step is to fill it up with hanging folders and label them accordingly. There are many methods of filing within a task drawer. The suggestions below are placed in order from most to least complexity.

- Within the business world, time management trainers teach the A to Z filing system for tasks. Over the years, I have recommended it to many home clients because it allows the space for integrating all open tasks regardless of what category of one's life the paper is needed. The caution with using it is that one would need to be very disciplined to always logging items on the task list appropriately. If you are selecting alphabetical order, use 26 hanging folders (any color) and label each file with one letter of the alphabet and hang in order from "A" to "Z."

- You can choose to file papers by the date that they are due or need to be worked on. If you are going to file by date you will need 31 hanging folders labeled 1 through 31. This will be your place to store papers that will be needed for tasks or calendar appointments on a particular date.

- Sometimes people think the above two options are too complicated and choose to use folders labeled "this week," "next week," "future months."

- If you want to be a little more open-ended and not associate a particular date to tasks, then you can utilize categories such as: phone calls to make, errands, data entry, and bills to pay. Please keep in mind, it is easier to miss deadlines when utilizing this method. You will need to be extra careful to make sure that your task book contains weekly entries to remind you to work on the tasks within the folders.

Remember you have to be comfortable with whatever system you use for categorizing the papers associated with tasks, so you have to select the system that works for you. If you don't know which one is best and it is too overwhelming to choose, start with creating one labeled "this week." If you chose this then every week you will have to go through ALL papers in the folder and decide what you are going to accomplish that week. Later, you can switch to a combination of any of the other methods. Knowing that the hardest can be toned down, the examples in this book will be based upon utilizing the alphabetical labeling system of tasks in the task drawer.

✂ Tool: Work-In-Progress (WIP) Area

Sometimes, the materials that you need to complete tasks are larger than paper. Some examples are clothing to be mended, repairs, pictures to be framed and gifts to be wrapped. Find an area where you can store these items temporarily until you can complete them. This area can be anywhere but should be large enough to store bulky items. One shelf is preferable so that the number of items can be limited and will not pile up.

Often you may have to complete a task, but the amount of space allocated may not be appropriate or large enough to hold the item. For example, Christmas gifts alone could take an entire shelf and may need to be stored in a separate location. Or you may need to fix an item that would be better stored in the garage. If this is the case, simply keep the item in the location where it is best suited but make a note of the task associated with it. The entry on Task List should be marked to remind yourself of the location in which the items are stored. We will refer to this as the "Work-In-Progress" (WIP) area.

✂ Tool: Temporary Backlog Area

The temporary backlog area is a space for you to start placing the piles of paper that have accumulated throughout your living space. It may also be a place to gather your incomplete projects. I find that many people have categories of incomplete projects. Some have knitting or sewing projects. Others have pictures to frame. While others have items to repair. At this point, just designate an area and mentally block off a section for papers and "non-papers." Label the areas to hold you accountable to move everything there.

Putting It All Into Action

Now that you have all of the tools ready to go, you are ready to put them into action! Start today and funnel your inputs into the inbox. Use this system for all new inputs. Do not worry about the clutter piles or backlog yet. This is where people fail because they are overwhelmed by the amount of paper and items they have already and get stuck by it. ***Start the system beginning today and go forward.***

If you can't get focused because there is too much of a backlog, then start this process by moving the clutter to the backlog area. It could take hours of man-power to haul everything to the designated backlog area. So be prepared for the physical task. I warn that the backlog area may get crowded very quickly. You may need to apportion another area for backlog. Just remember to separate paper vs non-paper. It will be easier later.

📌 **Tactic: <u>Using the Inbox</u>**

All incoming paper goes in one place – the inbox. Mail, notices from organizations, scraps of paper with reminders or phone numbers, receipts, newspapers, and magazines are just some examples. If you are a parent, it could include permission slips to sign or homework papers to check. It is important to train all people in your household to put items into the inbox and inform the inbox manager (you) if there is something that needs immediate attention. For example, if a child puts his homework into the inbox and the homework needs to be signed by the morning, you will need to make sure that you handle that immediately. Don't be tempted to place time-sensitive and voluminous papers like homework in a separate box. The point is that all of it should be handled every day. By handling it, I mean to act upon the urgent and file the less urgent for completing later. You want to learn to deal with time-sensitive items now and file others to be handled later. Keep reading you will learn what to do with the "handle later" items.

You never know what you will find in your inbox. One day I was sorting through my inbox and found a paper with an outline of a shoe. Upon investigation, I learned that my mother had asked my son to trace his current shoe and send it to her so she could get him new sneakers. So I guess sometimes things get in there by "Grandma's Orders."

Creating reminder notes is a great way to slow down. Whenever you think of something you have to do, write it on a note paper and put the note in the inbox. Remember the inbox is the funnel for your inputs. You will learn to control them later.

Sometimes the items that are too big to put into the inbox come into your sphere of responsibility and you do not want to forget that you have to complete a task with or for them. Write a reminder note that you have to do the task and write "WIP" on the note so you know where you put the item, then put the item in the WIP area that you have already created.

It is helpful to make **rules about putting items into the inbox**. In a way, this is pre-sorting inputs to make decision-making easier. Here are a few to get you started.

⇧ ***Do not put items in the inbox that can be discarded.***

If time permits, you can do a pre-sort of mail entering the inbox. If you have one minute, discard "junk" mail. About two-thirds of the mail you receive is most likely advertisements, flyers, and circulars. Unless you will use them this week or next week, throw them right in the recycle bin. If you receive a catalog, make a ten-second decision if you will use it within the next month. If you will not need it, take five seconds to tear out the address to shred and throw the catalog into the recycle bin.

⇧ ***Do not put items in the inbox that need attention from someone else.***

If you want to minimize the number of inputs going into the inbox you can make rules for the types of items that should go into it. Paper that does not need your attention or that needs to be managed by someone else should not go in your inbox.

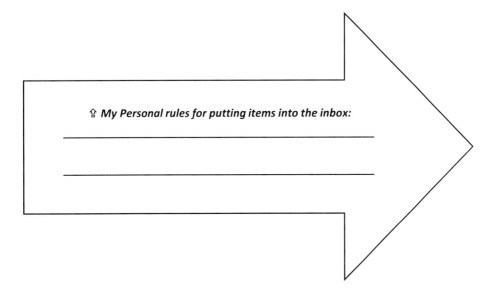

⇧ ***My Personal rules for putting items into the inbox:***

_____

_____

🔖 Tactic: <u>Listing Tasks on the Task List</u>

As a starting point, use the **Tasks - Now** and the **Tasks - Future** worksheets to begin listing the tasks that you know that need to be done. "Now" would be used for anything urgent or important. Future would be used for tasks that you need or want to complete but they don't have an urgency to them. An example of a future task would be a flyer for a store you want to try out but you don't necessarily need anything there.

1. In pencil, write down a task as appropriate on either list. Do not use pen. It will leave too much room for messiness. You should write just one item per task line.

2. If there is a paper associated with the task, file the paper in the appropriate task area: Task Drawer, WIP, or Backlog.

3. Then label in parentheses on the task list the location of papers associated with the task. It is easy to catch the eye if you put the location of the item in parentheses. For example, file papers associated with the task in the Task Drawer. If you are using the alphabetical system, how do you know what letter to file the paper under? Select one that makes sense to you. Whatever you choose, it is important to note on the task list where you filed the item for ease of retrieval later. For example, you have to call the exterminator and have a flyer with the phone number and other information. File the flyer under "E" for exterminator. The task you would write on your task list would be written as: Call Exterminator (E). Some other examples are mail packages (hall table) or fill out form (F) or mend curtains (WIP).

4. The last step is to select a date. When using the **Tasks– Now** and **Tasks– Future** worksheets write next to the task itself, the estimated date that you want to complete this task. When you are using the weekly task list, they will already be associated with a date that is written at the top of the sheet. When selecting a date, use the date that you may be able to start working on the task item not when it is due.

   Selecting a date can strike terror in the heart because you are telling yourself to commit to a deadline. Since you are writing in pencil, you will be able to move items to other days. You will eventually have about thirty days' worth of task items at any one time and for inputs requiring a larger time frame, you will learn to distribute tasks accordingly.

Tasks – Now

Priority	Task	Date

Tasks – Future

Priority	Task	Date

When you begin the process of "Putting Myself First," you will learn the intricacies of this system. For now, just keep everything on one of the two lists. Eventually, as you get more caught up on backlog, you will be able to create daily task lists, as opposed to lists labeled "Now" and "Future ."

Once you look at the list of "Future tasks" or papers in the "read" folder, you may notice that there are items on the list that are not relevant to who you are as a person. Imagine taking items OFF your task list for any or all of the following reasons:

- They do not need to be done today
- They do not need to be done at all
- They are just busywork
- They are not important to who you are as a human being
- They can be done by someone else.

This leaves NOTHING for you to do! You are done! Terrific! Enjoy the sensation of a heavy load sliding off your shoulders.

Of course, this is unrealistic. There will be stuff that has to be done today, is important, or can't be delegated. And you always have routine task items like preparing a healthy dinner, take a bath, and rest your body so it will be prepared for the day's work. Then if you are a self-actualizing human, you may add items that will help you grow spiritually. But here is the good news. You don't have to do it ALL in one day.

Tactic: Clearing the Inbox

Now that you have collected all of the inputs needing attention, it is time to learn how to prepare them for completion. In a manufacturing environment, this is called "staging." This staging process consists of setting aside time every day to clear out the papers in your inbox and decide when you will do the tasks associated with them. This does not mean you have to act on every paper during this staging process. You do have to decide what has to be done and when you are going to do it.

The ideal outcome for this stage is to empty all items of the inbox and put them either into one of the temporary storage areas until you have time to work on them or if no further action is needed, put them into permanent or long term storage. The temporary storage area is either the Task Drawer, WIP area, or Backlog area. At this point, we have not set up a long-term storage system. So if there is an item or piece of paper that requires long-term storage, put it into the Backlog Area within a box labeled "File for Reference." You will revisit this box when you start to "Lighten Your Load."

The rule is

⇧ ***Do not put anything in one of the Temporary Storage locations without noting the associated task on the task list.***

On average, the staging process only takes 15 minutes a day. This 15-minute step can save hours of inefficiency looking for scraps of paper or trying to decide what to do. If you skip a day, then plan 15 minutes times the number of days you have skipped this step. For example, if you only do this process once per week, then plan about two hours (15 minutes times seven days in a week equals one hour and 45 minutes). It is ok to skip a day or two but if you miss more, it can become overwhelming. At minimum, you should complete this Clearing out the inbox phase at least once per week.

The process is as follows:

1. Touch each paper once and decide what to do with it.

⇧ **Decide on paperwork immediately.**

Stop and think about the sentence above. Take time to process what you just read. This is a biggie. Deciding on each piece of paper or new input once it touches your hand or eyes is the biggest way you can get control of your life. In other words, this is a rule that you need to embrace!

2. If the paper does not need action, decide if you will need the paper again.

   a. If yes, it should be filed in long-term storage. For now, put the items in the box labeled "File for reference."

   b. If the paper does not need action and you will not need the paper again, toss or shred it.

3. If the paper needs action, then enter the task on the task list. When writing a task on the task list, it is important to be as specific as you need to remember what you have to do. Don't forget to note where you filed the item for ease of retrieval later. Some of the reminders that you put in your inbox may be notes with information that you need to refer to later. As you are clearing your inbox, just like with other papers, you need to decide if these notes are for reference and should be in a long-term storage location or if they will require action at a later date. For example, a note with a password might be for reference that would need to be filed in a permanent file whereas a note with a book that you may want to read would be a more temporary note and should be filed in the Task Drawer.
During this stage, the following rule applies.

⇧   *Enter all tasks from all sources into one place – your Task List.*

4. There is a middle group of papers and tasks that are neither junk mail that can quickly be discarded without reading nor are they in need of immediate handling. These are undecided category, any material for which you can't make a 30-second decision to keep. These represent papers or tasks that you are not sure need action. Some examples within this category are financial statements, investment information, communication company offers, catalogs which contain items that you MAY need to purchase, retirement information, government documents regarding social security, town meeting notices, and coupons we MAY use. Although this next suggestion might give permission to be indecisive, I still recommend it. **Create an additional hanging file in your task drawer labeled "read" or "decide."** If using this type of folder, you will need to still list this entire folder as a task to process and read the items. If you find that this folder is bulging within days, you may need to limit reading inputs. Write on the folder a guiding statement or key question to ask before deciding to read or not read. For example, ask will reading this help me be a better person? Then read these notes and questions BEFORE the item is placed into the folder.

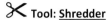 **Tool:** <u>Shredder</u>

You do not need to spend a lot of money on a shredder. For the average household a small under the desk six-sheet shredder is sufficient. When purchasing a shredder, the most important feature is "micro cross-cut." If you do not get this type, identity thieves can very easily re-create your information.

A Note about Shredding: Besides being fun, shredding creates complete closure on paper decision-making. The paper is never going to re-circulate in a maelstrom of clutter. You don't have to shred everything. Keep in mind that you should shred anything with your name or account number. So you don't have to shred an entire document, rip the address and account information off envelopes and magazines and shred only that portion.

📺 **Electronic Considerations:** <u>Clearing out the e-mail inbox</u>

To clear out the E-mail inbox, the goal is the same. The steps are similar as described above. Enter the task that needs to be completed onto the Task List. If you are using an electronic Task List that is integrated with the E-mail, then simply drag the e-mail to Task and it will create a new task. Now decide what to do with the original e-mail. You can file the entire e-mail in your permanent e-mail reference files or print out details needed from the e-mail and file it with the appropriate paper file, or delete it.

If you have many e-mails relating to one project you can create a subfolder within the inbox for the e-mails related to the uncompleted task. This is like the Task Drawer for electronic files. The task still needs to be listed on the Task List and needs to be referenced in the subfolder. This is not a permanent file. When the project is complete, the folder needs to be purged and e-mails that are being saved should be moved to a "completed" folder within the e-mail system. The ultimate goal is to purge as soon as possible so the E-mail Inbox does not get overwhelming.

🖈 Tactic: Grouping Routine Tasks

Even if you chose one of the other task drawer folder systems, in some cases, it may be easier to categorize similar tasks into one folder. In this case, you would schedule a time to work on that group of tasks at the same time. Some examples of the tasks that are often grouped are:

- Read
- Phone calls
- Forms to Fill out
- Items to enter into calendar
- Bills to Pay
- Data entry into contact database or phone
- Errands

If you are going to categorize any tasks, create a folder for all papers in that category. The same rule applies to this generalized task. ***Do not put anything in one of the Temporary Storage locations without writing the task to be completed on the task list.*** Create a task on the Task List for the *category*, write in parentheses the location that it is filed, and file the paper or item in the appropriate folder or WIP location.

🖈 Tactic: Staging Inputs on which there are Multiple Tasks

If you have a paper that includes many tasks but does not have the time to enter them all into the Task List, enter one task that will remind you to break out tasks associated with that paper and then file the paper in Task Drawer. For example, you may have gone to a meeting at which you had several follow up tasks. The task would read as follows: *Follow up on Meeting Notes* (M).

The project planning worksheet from the Simplify chapter is an example of multiple tasks on one input. As a practice, gather the paperwork that you created in the SIMPLE chapter and file it in the "P" folder. On your task list write: *Plan Project Timeline* (P).

📌 Tactic: <u>Handling Inputs that Others Owe You</u>

Before you can move ahead on a project, sometimes another person needs to accomplish a task or get back to you or return something to you. It is difficult to keep track of other people's commitments to you. To help with this, create a manila folder titled "Waiting for Reply" and then file it inside the hanging folder labeled "W." Finally create a task on your Task List to follow up with the person (W).

Now you have narrowed your inputs into two places.

1. **Task list** which references the task drawer or area. With this list, you know what needs to be done and where the items needed to do it are located.
2. **Task drawer (or WIP Area)** which, in an organized way, stores the items needed to do the tasks so you can retrieve them easily when you ready to do them.

📌 Tactic: <u>Staging Backlog</u>

You are equipped with the tools to live a slower simpler life. However, you may have piles of paper and/or mounds of possessions that have previously been accumulated. You may have so much backlog that you cannot see the light at the end of the tunnel or the bottom of the pile. ***Don't let this backlog stop you from moving forward.***

This process of handling backlog is where "slow down" comes into play. You need to slow down and not take on any new projects or tasks so that you have time to process the ones that you already have in the works. You may be saying to yourself: Life seems to carry in new projects anyway. Yes it does, but you can be selective which ones you accept.

To get through the backlog follow the steps below. These will sound easier to accomplish than they really are.

1. Schedule time to process backlog. There is no getting around it. You will need to schedule additional chunks of time to whittle down the already existing piles. Even if you are only able to schedule one hour a week, it is better than nothing. You can hire a professional organizer to help you plow through the masses but ultimately you will still need to make many decisions.

2. Process the backlog in stages. For example, start with the kitchen table. Once you have mastered that area then you can work on another area with confidence and more energy because you can see success.

3. Create rules of engagement for handling backlog. Start with the rules created for putting an item in the inbox. If under the new system you would not put something in it, then discard it.

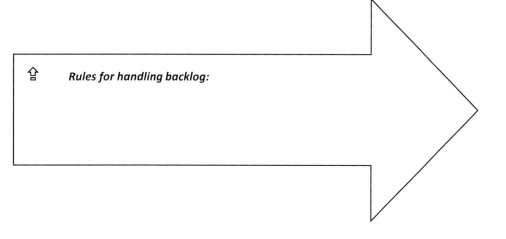

Rules for handling backlog:

4. Once you work on an area and find tasks that need attention, follow the same process. Write the task onto the Task list and, if there is an associated item, file the item in the task drawer or WIP area.

As you are working your way through your backlog, time will pass and you may need to accomplish tasks that were previously listed on the "Tasks - Future" list. It is perfectly normal to move items to the "Tasks – Now." The "Tasks - Future" may need rewriting several times before you complete the process. Conversely, some of the tasks on the list may end up remaining on your list for months and the associated items may be collecting dust on the WIP shelf. At some point, you are going to have to evaluate all of your tasks to see if they are still worth doing. In other words, at least once a year go through your task list and corresponding drawer, folders, or shelf and see if the task is still important to keep on your list. I suggest using your birthday as a trigger for that task.

During this time of transition, it is essential to continue to keep up with the new inputs for current responsibilities or projects.

♀ Taking it Deeper

Up until this point, we have been looking at the external ways to help you slow down. However, sometimes rushing around is a ploy by our subconscious minds to avoid learning about ourselves. When you slow down, you tend to find out who you are, and if you truly know yourself.

All people have a set of underlying beliefs, whether they consciously recognize them or not. There are about three or four essential beliefs unique to each person that make up a person's core. You may think there are more but when you search yourself you only have a few central themes to your life. As people progress throughout life, they meet others who share one or more of their core beliefs. Some people will overlap one or two of your core values, but not all. It is okay that people overlap to different degrees. The more core beliefs shared between people the more likely that they will be closer to you and be in each other's life for a longer period of time.

To help you begin (or continue) to understand who you are and what you like, fill out the **Observation Questions** about yourself. It will get you thinking about who you really are. This list is only a beginning to get you thinking. If you would like to do more of this type of exploration, many books will give you further tools and resources for personal wisdom.

My Favorite...

TV program	_____	Musical artist	_____
Movie	_____	Place	_____
Magazine	_____	Game as a child	_____
Hobby	_____	Hero at age 10	_____

One word to describe me is... _____

A challenge in my life right now is... _____

_____

I wish I had more time for…

_____

_____

I am inefficient in ways such that…

_____

_____

I would like to participate in…

_____

_____

I wish people would…

_____

_____

It takes too long to…

_____

_____

When it comes to making a tough decision I generally (check one)

___ struggle for days	___ make a snap decision
___ wait to see what else might happen	___ ask for advice
___ hope it will go away	___ take a walk
___ never had a tough decision	

In times of trouble, I tend to rely on (check one)

___ myself	___ family
___ God	___ my friends
___ my teacher	___ one friend
___ anyone around me	

As you move through the journey of life, you will be presented with opportunities, challenges, and choices. Sometimes, these diversions may cause you to lose focus and make decisions that you may regret. Use the **About Me Worksheet** to create a one-page touchstone that you can use to remind yourself what is important. Or if necessary carry a short mission statement with you and read over it from time to time. It will help you locate your core during busy or deeply stressful times when you are less able to make clear decisions.

If you are open to self-development, each new experience will help you understand yourself a little better. Buy a **notebook or journal** (✂) to write down personal lessons that

you learn so you can refer to your solutions when necessary.

When you begin to honor your true nature, you will have less need for time-management because you will instinctively select activities and people that are in tune with who you are. In other words, you will be Un-managing your time.

The bottom line remains. Slow Down so you can learn more about yourself and live a life more consistent with who you are meant to be.

About Me

My mission in life is...

My skills are...

⏱ Quick Hits

- **Practice sitting.**

  Not playing a game or reading or knitting. Just sitting. When sitting, notice the way the light falls in the room. Or the scent of the air. Notice your surroundings. Be aware. Go back to the **Clear the Clutter in Your Mind Exercise** (✂ **Activity p.** 17) as many times as necessary until it becomes second nature.

- **Single-tasking.**

  Do not try to do more than one task at a time. Select a more important one and give it your full attention. You really do not have too much to do. It is an illusion that you create. Think of each task and ask what is important. Are you making food for someone to show them you love them? Why not just spend time with them instead.

- **Listen.**

  When being with a person, listen to what the other person is trying to say. Often people listen to the beginning of another's thought and assume where the person is taking the thought or the point the person is trying to make. A counseling technique is to repeat what the person says to make sure you understand. The joke I heard is: "Do you need me to be part of this conversation or do you have it covered?"

- **Smile and appreciate.**

  Yes, you probably already appreciate the people who make a difference in your daily life but why not appreciate everything that comes your way? Walk past something and let it know you appreciate it. Hello tree in my yard! Thank you for providing shade for my family, all year, not just in the summer.

Chapter 4: 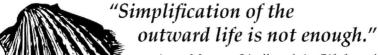 Get Introspective

> *"Simplification of the outward life is not enough."*
> — Anne Morrow Lindbergh in *Gift from the Sea*

In this chapter, we will explore what it means to "get introspective." When I came up with the S.I.M.P.L.E. acronym, I could have used other words that begin with the letter "I" such as integrate or interdependent or even important. But getting introspective is the strategy that will allow the internal space for the large scale or "macro" planning necessary to be truly organized for life.

If you want to be successful in this journey of life organization, you should commit to being reflective of yourself, your relationships with people as well as your activities, and your responsibilities. Concerning the topic of time, you should commit to becoming very familiar with how you spend your time and learn to recognize the superfluous tasks that are taking away from your ability to live the life you are seeking.

What kinds of choices have you made about your life? How have they affected your ability to allocate your energies? Do you make your decisions out of habit or conscious choice? Did you just eat that candy bar because it is a habit or did you consciously think about how your body will react when it is eaten, both on your tongue as well as your heart and hips? When you have to get up early for a business trip, do you still go to bed at midnight to watch the late show, out of habit? Whether or not your choices are conscious and rational, they do shape who you are today.

If you are going to make progress with life organization and ultimately life balance, you will need to start making more conscious decisions with your time and start changing your habits to be in line with your new ways of thinking. Look at the questions on the **Personal**

Choices Questions and begin thinking about the choices you have already made to get you to where you are today. These questions are designed to be thought-provoking. Use the space, or additional paper if necessary, to write brief answers that you can look back upon and remind yourself that you have made personal decisions in your life and that you must live with their consequences.

- What nutritional choices do I make as far as the foods I eat?

- What steps do I take for my outward appearance?

- What type of family situation do I have?

- What type of work do I perform?

- What type of transportation do I use to get to work? Elsewhere?

- What type of area do I live in?

- What size and type of house do I have?

- What quality of furnishings do I own?

- How many belongings do I have that I need in my life?

- How much money do I need to provide the quality of life I choose?

- How much effort do I put into my spiritual growth?

Did you like the answers to these questions? Have you been making choices that are consistent with your views of life? I ask myself those questions often. Sometimes when I start on a path of introspection, I drive myself crazy. I debate with myself on the why of something. Whatever the topic or issue of the day, I may ask myself whether it is my personality or the way I was raised. There are so many possibilities of why but more importantly since this book is about organizing, let's look at how being an organized person with manageable inputs and tasks will ultimately allow the time to explore the whys.

🖈 Tactic: <u>Reflect on Life</u>

Sit quietly with yourself every day to examine your thoughts, feelings, and beliefs. Go ahead and experience your emotions. Feel them. Write about them. Laugh at yourself. Cry. Don't be afraid to experience the emotions once you let them out, you will feel better. It is normal. You are not weird for having them.

🖈 Tactic: <u>Know your Limitations</u>

Part of getting introspective includes knowing and liking yourself as well as understanding your physical limitations.

> To illustrate this point, my colleague shared the following story.
>
> In my job, it is common for me to work ten hours a day, five days a week on a keyboard typing seventy wpm. I had carpal tunnel surgery on one wrist, and shortly afterward had similar surgery on the other wrist. Both times, I tried going back to work the day after release from surgery and ignored the pain in my wrists. In the end, it was a disaster. My hands felt like they were on fire every day and I kept having to slow down and stop working. Worse, my actions set back my recovery, forced me to cancel a trip to see my son, and inconvenienced my coworkers. Ultimately, I ended up taking six weeks off to let both wrists heal properly.

It's great to push the boundaries but you will do more damage in the long term if you push too hard. Recognize that you cannot be a superhuman who does everything. A good rule of thumb is if it hurts physically, mentally, or emotionally, STOP. Often the people I work with have admitted that they physically can't lift or get tired doing tasks for too long. Others have recognized that decision-making is fatiguing or the objects we are sorting hold emotional baggage. Hurray for them. What about you? You may not need to be a professional organizer to accomplish tasks but you need to learn to pace yourself and work within your boundaries.

When confronted with a request for your time you must be able to know if you are capable of fulfilling it. It may not always be physical or mental limitations. It may be a limitation due to your responsibilities. Sometimes you may have the knowledge and the willingness, but other things are taking priority.

⇧ Plan only 40% of your time.

When I was first learning about time management, it was common for my teachers to reference the Pareto principle, the 80/20 rule. This states that for many events, roughly 80% of the effects come from 20% of the causes. This rule has been applied to almost every discipline. In time management it has been used to teach others to schedule 80% of their day, leaving room for 20%.

So why have I chosen 40%? Because I know that planning 80% is very rigid and does not allow a person the spontaneity to take advantage of the opportunities that come along. What if your day was so packed, that you missed the opportunity to get a call from your long lost cousin? Or that you did not have the time to truly appreciate the effort your child put into a school project?

There is one school of thought that reminds people to heed not only the messages from others but from animals and plants that are showing up in your life. For example, seeing a hawk crossing your path can mean that there is something you cannot see and a hawk will help you in that.

No matter what percentage of your day you use for planning and how deeply you dive, it is good to plan no more than 80% of your day to allow time for unexpected things that will come along.

🎣 Tactic: <u>Get Introspective with your Actions</u>

Are you constantly running from one activity to the next without experiencing any of them fully? Do you have too many interests and cannot choose which one to work on in a given day? Are you afraid of missing something? If you answered "yes" to any of the above questions, maybe you are trying to do too much. Maybe you are doing activities that are presented to you without giving any thought to the quality of the activities, or their meaning in your life.

Get introspective with your actions. In other words, think about your actions and strive to do fewer and more meaningful activities. Over the long term of your life, the more you push, the more depleted of energy you will be. If you don't watch your actions, your ailments will overpower your daily living and you won't be able to complete all the tasks anyway. I had to learn this lesson the hard way. When I was in my twenties, I used to compete in triathlons. By the time I was twenty-six, I was done. I pushed myself so much that my body suffered. It has taken extra effort during the rest of my life to compensate for that damage and I am still not done.

Also, life is too short for being involved in activities and tasks that you do not enjoy. However, I don't want to give you permission to shrink daily responsibilities of simply living.

Washing your own dishes, tidying up your environment, and paying bills, for example, are non-negotiable. So **learn to enjoy the tasks associated with existence as a responsible human being on the planet.**

𝄞 Taking it Deeper

📌 Tactic: <u>Get Introspective About Others</u>

As we age, we naturally know more people than we did when we were younger and to keep up quality relationships takes time. I have an easy time talking with people so I naturally know many people. However, sometimes I ask myself permission to take a break from meeting people so I can further develop the relationships with people I already know. Other times, I think back on the people I have known and feel guilty for not continuing the relationship. To keep it up would have been work and time but at the time I didn't put in the effort. And still other times, I need to remember a child in a sandbox. I need to remind myself, it is okay to spend time with people in a particular moment and not have to make plans to ever see them again.

No matter which scenario applies to you, you will need to make choices regarding the amount of time you spend with which people. Developing meaningful relationships will take commitment.

Think of five people you enjoy spending time with. These should be people you really enjoy spending time with because they understand you and you understand them. They may be people who have taught you something worthwhile or helped you through a difficult time. They could be people who have made you feel appreciated and special or people that make you light at heart.

Do you regularly spend time with these people? Schedule time to be with one person with whom you want to strive for greater intimacy. When you are with that person, do activities together where you are truly learning about the person. Fill out the **Observation Worksheet** from the previous chapter about the other person. Then share your answers with each other.

Now go even deeper and explore the why of your answers. Many times people hold on to items or fill up their schedules so that they do not have to be close with others. Are you one of those people? Here are some questions to ask yourself:

- Am I afraid of being close to others?
- Have people let me down in the past?
- Do you always try to impress people?
- Do you have to work hard to meet another's expectations or to fit in with your friends?
- Do you feel devalued by people or let them manipulate you into traps such as guilt, anger, helplessness, or teasing?

⊕ Quick Hits

- **Spend one day a week in which you turn off all electronic devices.** This action forces you to be present and communicate more thoroughly with the people you are physically with at the time. It allows you the ability to not be thinking about other responsibilities or people.

- **Join groups that allow learning about yourself.** For example, if you belong to a church or synagogue, don't just attend worship. Get involved in one of the groups that meets outside of worship even if it is merely helping to plan a one-time event such as a fundraiser or concert.

- **Spend quality time with your partner or children to better get to know them.** Instead of a watching movie or playing a video game, do an activity that allows for more interaction. Going on a nature walk with them could be just the opportunity the other needs for sharing a concerning issue. Or playing an interactive board game could be just what the doctor orders.

- **Go to therapy or find another way to work through issues** such as giving yourself time to meditate, exercise, practice yoga, or attend a meditation, exercise, or yoga class at least once a week. When you go to these things on your own or in class, turn off your cellphone and leave it in another room or at home. Give yourself time to focus your entire mind on something else for an hour. Even if you cannot follow a guided meditation, use the time away from electronic devices and other people to focus on something that is bothering you.

- **Be a good friend**. If you don't know what a good friend is, learn. List the qualities you want in a friend and display those qualities to your friends.

- **Have fun without spending money** to show you what really matters. For example, have a picnic or create your own game.

- **Put yourself in situations that allow safe exploration of feelings.** Find friends that are not overly critical and allow you to be yourself.

- **Only spend time with people whose outlook on life is the same as yours.**

- **Quit some organized activities.** Quit the activities and decline the events that do not fit with the core values that you defined in the "About Me" exercise. The fewer activities in which you are involved means the more time you will have to enjoy the activities that you continue doing. This may mean you will come in less contact with people but hopefully, you will have better quality relationships with the people that are in your life.

- **Practice saying "no."** There is a scene in the movie "27 Dresses" where the main male character, Kevin, is trying to get the main female character, Jane, to practice saying "no." He has pointed out to her that she just can't say no when people ask her to do things, so he repeatedly asks to borrow fifty bucks and she keeps saying "no." Then he changes his tactic and says "I need you to give me 50 bucks." She is now starting to get worn down. "No," she says. Then he laughs and says "See? That was good." Then he picks up her drink and says "Jane, can I have your drink?" "Sure" is her reply. Next time someone asks you to help with something, ask yourself if you really want to do it or if you say yes just to be nice.

- **Perform only one task at a time.** Although you may think you are getting more done, your body and mind will eventually get tired. During a martial arts sparring match in which two people are trying to knock each other off balance, the one who continually defends his position without taking any action to overtake his opponent will eventually get so tired he will fall over. This is the same when you are trying to do too much at once. You are continually completing tasks to defend your position of having everything completed. Instead, do the tasks one at a time and enjoy the act of doing them.

Chapter 5 - Phase I - 🕸 Stabilize

Now that you have done the pre-work, you can get started on the organizing journey from macro to micro. Organization and the way to get there will look different for everyone. For some, as suggested previously, it could be slowing down to start the process. For others, it could be changing deep-rooted habits and still for others it could be getting the extraneous clutter out of the way to have the physical space to begin. No matter what your life circumstance, the first phase of the life organization process is: Stabilize.

The key component of stabilization is to create a starting point or plan. Please keep in mind that plans ALWAYS change. Even the best planners in the world have monkey wrenches thrown into the mix. You are wading into uncharted territory. As humans, we crave certainty, but this will be a time where you will be in transition. The plan will help guide you so you don't keep freefalling without a place to land.

A mistake that many chronically disorganized people make is to think that they can skip the stabilization phase. I have seen it over and over again where people want to skip the first two phases and start with the "organize" phase of the process. Stabilizing and prioritizing may be easy for some but the assumption is that since you are reading this book you need additional help.

Now is a good time for you to commit to the rules of engagement for the entire process. Please sign the following form as a commitment to yourself.

⌂ Life Organization Covenant With Self

Pre-Requisites:

I will slow down and allow the time necessary for the process.

I will get introspective to prepare myself for a successful outcome.

I will be open to eliminating the unnecessary.

Phase 1 – Stabilize

I will spend time determining what open tasks need to be completed for stabilization.

I will not engage in new activities or outside processes while in this phase.

Phase 2 – Prioritize

I will create an initial plan of tasks with corresponding priorities.

Phase 3 – Organize

I will update my project plan as tasks are completed or related details are identified.

I will add organizing rules as new ones are determined.

Phase 4 – Transition

I will continue to remain organized.

I will strive for balance every day.

I hereby agree to these rules and commit to follow them on my journey towards life organization.

Signed: _____

Date: _____

🖈 Tactic: Macro planning

Before you start the tactics of scheduling how to spend your time and hopefully stabilize how you utilize your energy, you need to go through a process of macro planning. On a high level, it is strategizing what you are trying to accomplish and includes setting guidelines that will aid during the actual process.

A **macro** sort is one in which you separate something into broad categories. In this chapter the "something," to use as an example, will be paper. It will be simple. Is the paper needed for a current task to be completed or is it needed to retain for reference? Then the sorting process will move on to the macro sort of items where you will be planning the categories needed to contain your possessions. Then in the *Lighten Your Load* chapter, you will physically macro sort the items. At this stage, you are just planning.

Zone defense is a sports reference best known in basketball. For this game, there are always five players for each team on the court. When the ball is on the side of the court in which the team is defending the hoop, a coach may choose to have players use a zone defense. This strategy dictates that a player covers a particular area of the court no matter who enters it. Similarly, a zone defense in organizing means to create areas specifically designated for functions.

In the *Slow Down* chapter, you examined inputs (i.e. verbal requests written on scraps of paper, papers, or items) related to a task that needs to be completed. In essence, you began the sorting process of inputs and started to sort what you used to call chaos. Now in this phase, you should take time to become familiar with what types of possessions you own, what tasks you have to complete, and the items are needed to complete them.

Don't get too overzealous. You still won't be immersing yourself in the nitty-gritty yet. It is time to do a large scale or macro planning and rule setting. Eventually, the process will add how to work projects into your day. For now, I am suggesting using some current paperwork as practice on how the system will work. Still don't try to tackle any backlog or big projects until you fully understand the process.

🔖 Tactic: Macro Sort the Task List

Let's get started by eliminating the tasks that are not urgent. It is too easy to ignore the tasks that have to be done to learn something new or focus on a more rewarding project. But you can't lose sight of current responsibilities. Taking time to embrace this macro planning is what will encourage stabilization and ultimately success.

Start by pulling out the previously created "**Task List – Now**."

1. Look at it to see if there are **duplicates**. If yes, combine them. Make sure to combine any paperwork associated with the task.

2. See if anything can be **deleted**. Tasks would be deleted if, when evaluating them, they are no longer relevant to you, have been completed or are no longer important. If removing something from the list, discard any paperwork or item associated with the deleted task.

3. Pull out the "**Tasks- Future**" list and re-evaluate the tasks listed to see if any need to be moved to the "Tasks – Now" list. If yes, **transfer the identified tasks to the "Tasks - Now"** list. On the "Tasks - Future," in the small box to the left-most column of the moved task write an arrow (->). This signifies that you have moved the task. Re-file the "Tasks- Future" list into the task file.

4. Look at the "Tasks – Now "and begin to **macro prioritize** the tasks by writing an "A" or "B" in the priority column of the list. Note, the A's and B's do not need to be written in order of importance.

   To determine if a task is an "A" priority use the following guidelines:

   - It is for a current project or responsibility
   - In general, it needs to be done within the next three months.

   To determine if a task is a "B" priority use the following guidelines:

   - It is not for a current project or responsibility.
   - It does not need to be done within the next three months.

5. Re-write all of the "B" priority tasks onto a new, **second "Tasks – Future."** On the "Tasks– Now" list, in the small box to the left of the task moved put an arrow (->). This means you have moved the task. File the "Tasks – Future" into the Task Box in

the folder labeled "Q" for next quarter. On your "A" task list add the following as a task: "Quarterly Planning (Q). This will remind you to revisit the list in two and a half months. However, until the end of the quarter you may end up moving items back to the "A" list but until the time comes for you to work on a given task you shouldn't worry about all of the other tasks that were on the "B" list.

Now for the next three months, you only have to concentrate on completing the "A's." Does it seem less overwhelming already? Now brace yourself for beginning on the backlog box of paperwork previously created and called "File for Reference."

✎ Tactic: Macro Sort Papers

For this exercise, you can collect any pile of papers and use them as an example for the Macro Sort. Find a pile of papers in the house that has not been touched in a while. If you don't think you have one, I guarantee you will find one. Some places to look are table next to the television, kitchen cabinet, above laundry area, desk, car, bedroom closet, night table in the bedroom, and the entryway table.

✂ Tool: Paperwork Decision Flowchart

Use the **Paperwork Decision Flowchart** included in this chapter to help with decision-making. It was designed for one of my clients who was having trouble making decisions about paperwork. Since I use it so often to help break down the decision-making process, I found it necessary to include. The process is very simple - hold a piece of paper in your hand and determine if an action is needed. In other words, should an associated task with the paper be put on the task list? If yes, write the task on the list and file the paper in the appropriate letter within the task drawer. If no, then ask if the paper will be needed again. If no, trash, shred or recycle it. If yes, then one more set of decisions needs to be made. Does the paper already have a home or not?

PAPERWORK DECISION FLOWCHART

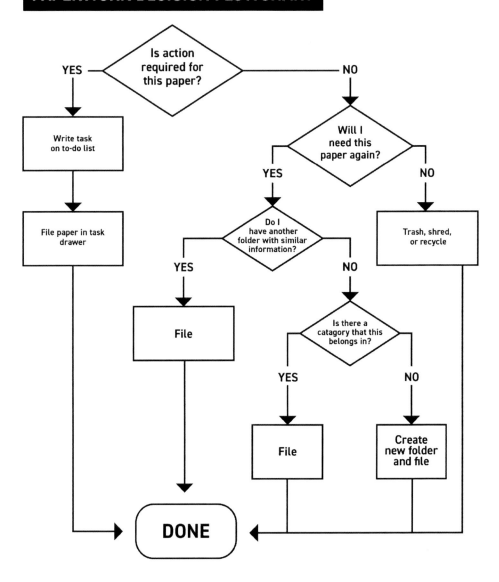

1. **Have a Home.**

    Home is defined as a location designated specifically for a particular item. For paper, the home is usually a filing cabinet or binder. A pile on the desk or kitchen table is not considered a home. You may think, I am saying out in the open is not a home because it looks messy, but there is more to it. Every time you walk by the pile you subconsciously think about the tasks that need to be done which diminishes your energy.

    You may already have files created. The question to ask is: Do I have another folder with similar information. If no, then ask if there is another folder with a similar category.

2. **Have No home.**

    If a paper has no home, it means that you do not already have a clearly marked folder or binder in which it can be stored. If you do not have another folder with similar information, don't worry, we will get there. You are not going to do more with these piles right now.

How to file papers will be addressed in the *Lighten Your Load – Information* chapter. The purpose of this exercise was to teach you how to sort large piles into smaller ones that are not so daunting. Three easy questions about paperwork which can be expanded to all items:

- Is Action required?
- Is it needed again?
- Where should it be stored?

To store these papers out of the way, put them in separate cardboard boxes clearly labeled with the category. The "Have a Home" box should be labeled "file-information." The "Have No Home" box should be labeled "Create new folder." You may have multiple boxes for each of the categories.

You may be asking, why don't we just file these now? It seems like an extra step. You are correct but you cannot get distracted by doing the task until you understand how to break things down into parts. By skipping over this critical step, you would be setting yourself up to stay with the same old habits while the piles will continue to grow without an end in sight. This is the part of the journey from macro to micro. Macro organizing is learning to see the big picture in which you must learn to determine categories. In other words, you need the zone defense.

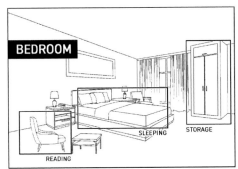 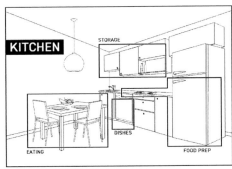

♣ Tactic: Macro Categorization of Items

✂ Activity: <u>The Zone Defense</u>

You are already using this system in part of your life. If someone was to ask you "Where do you keep your bread?", you would be able to say definitively it is in the refrigerator or bread cupboard. You have also started a zone defense outside of the refrigerator by creating a zone for paperwork. Congratulations! Now, look at the rest of your physical space.

Use the **Zone Organizing Worksheet** to list the zones for your personal zone defense. This worksheet is designed to list the zones that you need in your life but seeing that vision is not always clear. Rather than think about what you want, it may be easier to start with the spaces that you already have in your home and/or office. Give a critical eye to look at what the area was originally intended for and what it is actually being used for. Do not be afraid to deem obsolete some zones that you may no longer need. For example, if you have a zone for your skiing supplies but have not skied in years, there may be no need to have a zone for that task or maybe plan to make it a part of your life again.

Zone Organizing

Task	Zone	Items

Another approach is to determine the general tasks within your everyday routines and identify the zones associated with them. For example, in the kitchen you need cooking supplies, food, serving supplies, and dish cleaning supplies.

The technique that I most often use to determine zones needed is to make note of the types of items in a particular space. When looking at the space, I determine the large or macro categories.

See the following for some ideas.

Task	Zone	Items
Eating	Kitchen/Dining Room	Dishware, Mats, Napkins, Utensils, Glassware
Sleeping	Bedroom	Clock radio, Lamp
Exercising	Recreation Room or Outdoors	Mat, DVD
Cleansing	Bathroom	Towels, Soap, Personal care items, Toothbrush
Dressing	Bedroom/Closet	Clothes, Shoes, Jewelry
Storing	Attic/Basement/ Closet/ Garage	Out of season items, Overstock
Processing Paperwork	Office	Desk, Files
Recreation	Den/Living Room	Sofa, Fireplace, Game table, Lamp, TV, DVD, Stereo
Driving	Corner/ Wall	Hook or container for keys, Purse, Wallet, Vehicle
Pet	Kitchen	Pet dishes, Food

Task	Zone	Items
Laundry	Laundry room/Hamper/ Basement	Baskets, Detergents, Folding table
Work	Office	Desk, Phone, Calendar
Study / research	Library	Shelves, Table, Books, Paper, Pen
Transitioning	Hall/Living Room	Chair or small table, Bench, Mirror, Bills, Library books

Now that you have a guideline for the zones you need, sorting your belongings will become infinitely easier. For now, if you must, go ahead and get your hands dirty; move items into the proper zone. But I warn you, you may get discouraged when you start realizing how many items you own within each category. Do not give attention to the overflow of items within each zone. Just determine what the zones are.

Also, do not try to sort items into micro categories within the zone. For example, writing utensils are the macro category where pens, pencils, markers, or crayons would be the micro categories. The details of sub-dividing into micro categories will come later in the *Lighten Your Load* Chapter.

✂ Activity: Needs Assessment

Presumably, the list that you created on the Zone Defense Worksheet was made with your preconceived ideal needs in mind. Now take a critical look at where you currently are with zones. Use the **Needs Assessment – Home** and **Needs Assessment – Business** to help you take a detailed look at your current zones. In this exercise, only complete the Y or N column. The priority column will be used later when dealing with priorities.

Needs Assessment - Home

Room	Areas to Check	Y/N	Priority
Kitchen	Counter and table tops clear		
	Oldest food less than 6 months old		
	No chipped plates or non-functional tools		
Living Room	Window areas clear of clutter		
	Tabletops have room for temporary items		
	Place to sit comfortably		
Bedrooms	Corners not blocked		
	Dirty laundry in closed container		
	All clothes worn within last year		
	Nothing under bed		
Bathroom	Counter Clear		
	Dirty laundry/towels in closed container		
Office	Clutter-free desk		
	Work surface clear		
	File cabinets organized and not too full		
	Computer files organized		
Garage	Space for seasonal items		
	Space for cars		
Exercise Area	Separate area or room for exercise		
	Equipment free of clutter		
Attic/Basement	Collections stored away or eliminated		
	Broken equipment staged for fixing		
	Old magazines/books not piled up		
Entryway/Foyer	Room for temporary items (keys, etc.)		
	Room for movement		
General	Heaters not blocked		
	Doors not blocked		
	No piles on stairs or in halls		

Needs Assessment – Business

Room	Areas to Check	Y/N	Priority
Task List	All in one place (no post it notes)		
	References items needed for tasks		
	Updated for the day		
	Location for future task items		
Desk	Clutter-free desk		
	Work surface clear		
	Place to sit comfortably to work		
Office	Everything has a home		
	Area for temporary items (i.e. keys, lunch)		
	Place for guests to sit comfortably		
	Doors, windows, and heaters not blocked		
Computer	Quick Information retrieval		
	Less than 10 items in e-mail inbox		
	Contact list organized – recent contacts		
	All applications are currently being used		
Filing	Small or no area for "to-be-filed"		
	File cabinets organized and not too full		
	System for archiving old files		
Business Plan	Clear business mission		
	Documented five year plan		
	Clear yearly goals		
Finances	Clear cash flow & accounting procedures		
	Regular schedule for bill paying		
	Expense reporting up to date and accurate		
Processes	Workflow is clear to everyone		
	There are no clogs in the process		
Storage	Collections stored away or eliminated		
	Broken equipment staged for fixing		
	No outdated equipment		

With these two activities, you have spent the time to see where you are and where you want to go. Now you can begin to figure out how to get there. You do not have to do all of the sorting or detailed planning now, but you do have to write something on your Task List that serves as a reminder to continue sorting. On your master Task List, "Task List – Now", write the following task: "Create schedule of organizing (O)." In order to quickly retrieve these Needs Assessments and Zone Worksheets so you can remember what decisions you just made, file them in the "O" hanging folder.

🖥 Electronic Considerations: <u>E-Mail Zones</u>

Imagine an empty inbox at the end of a day and the e-mails that need response logged onto a task list ready to go for a future date. Clearing the inbox should be treated with the same process as that of clearing the paper inbox. That means e-mail filing should consist of two zones.

1. **E-mails that need action (incomplete).** Incomplete e-mails should either be dragged to the electronic task list. If there are many e-mails related to one outstanding project, incomplete e-mails should be moved to a sub-folder specifically created for the project. These folders should be treated as an electronic version of the Task Drawer. If a folder for a project has been created, do not forget to add a task onto the Task List which states "purge items from electronic project folder and move sub-folder to completed folder."

2. **E-mails that no longer require action (complete).** For the completed e-mails, create a Completed Folder with sub-folders by subject or topic and file retained e-mails accordingly.

⇧ Macro Organizing Rules

As part of the macro planning, I recommend that you set up rules of engagement for the physical organizing phase. This is different than the rules set forth in the covenant with yourself. They are meant to be the reminder of the global or macro decisions you make. If you don't write them down, they aren't real and you will forget them.

⇧ **Schedule no more than one, 2-4 hour time block per organizing session.**

Whenever you are working on a project you should spend an average of three hours per session. For some people, two hours will be sufficient and for others, four could work. However, you should do no longer than four hours because you will become fatigued and no shorter than two hours because you need at least that much time to get something completed. If your organizing project is mostly mental and emotional, then you should plan the two-hour time block. If it is mostly physical with very little hard decision-making then three hours is a good time frame. Finally, the four-hour time block should be reserved for sit down projects in which paperwork is being sorted at a macro level or computer records are being organized after the rules have been set. These are only guidelines and each person is different regarding their tolerance for each aspect of their world, but the recommendations are what has been common for most people.

⇧ **Drink water during the organizing process.**

Drink water during your session. I am guilty of forgetting to drink during a session. However, if I prepare a large container of water before the session and I forget during, it will be ready to consume in its entirety at the end of the session. Working on projects where there is a lot of paper or dust is especially dehydrating, so care should be taken to drink more water for those types of sessions.

⇧ Take a shower after each organizing session.

It may seem impractical, but shower after each organizing session. Even if you regularly use a house cleaner and you think you did not get dirty during the process, you did. You stirred up a lot and it needs to be cleaned from your body. On a deeper level, think of showering as a way to let go of all the baggage you have been holding onto.

Creating rules for categories of items you can part with will be very helpful. An easy one for example can be, "I can let go of all the clothing that is two sizes too small." Or another could be "I can give away the lawn tools since I no longer have a lawn." Use the categories identified during the zone defense process as a start for the rules related to categories. If you have trouble identifying categories, an objective person such as a professional organizer can help.

It is also important to make individualized rules for yourself. These should be WRITTEN DOWN to remind you of what you decided during a session so you won't have to go back and re-invent the wheel each time you start. For example, you could write: once a piece of paper is in the shred pile, I don't have to think about it again. Another that has been on several people's lists is: I will only keep a designated number of empty boxes (you choose the number) to be used for shipping or wrapping.

Finally, it is important to designate how long after a session you will remove items from your space and where you will take them. You may think you are making fantastic progress on making decisions about and purging items but if you do not commit to removing them from your property (or your car for those who have gone so far as to get them in the car), then you have not completed your task. You may need to schedule follow up sessions with yourself to remove the items.

Determining the personal rules may be a challenge but once you begin the actual lightening of your load, the ideas for macro rules should start becoming clear.

Utilize the **Macro organizing Rules** worksheet to add to the rules listed. Notice that this sheet has been started for you.

Macro Organizing Rules

⬆ Schedule no more than 2-4 hour time block per organizing session.

⬆ Drink water during the organizing process.

⬆ Take a shower after each organizing session.

Categories or general description of items that can be discarded:

_____   _____

_____   _____

_____   _____

_____   _____

_____   _____

My personal rules:

_____   _____

_____   _____

_____   _____

_____   _____

⬆ Bring donated items to _____ by _____ days after session.

I commit to these rules and will make a separate agreement for micro paperwork.

Signed _____

Date _____

Chapter 6: 🕸 Put Myself First

You may be thinking, "Great. I've done all this thinking and planning, how am I going to find time to do any of it?" In the *Slow Down* chapter, you looked at what you are currently committed to doing and where to put the items needed to do it. In the *Stabilize* chapter, you started making decisions about what needs to be done now. You have also decided where the items will be stored until you are ready for them. Now you can start taking control of your time and putting yourself first so you can begin taking action on the goals you set earlier.

Put yourself first does not mean to be selfish, nor does it mean to be inconsiderate of others. It means taking care of your own needs first so you have the capacity for whatever comes your way. The instruction given in case of an emergency on an airplane is to put a mask on yourself before trying to help others. This is what the phrase, "Put Myself First," means. Take care of yourself first so you are ready to help others and/or accomplish things.

📌 Tactic: Understanding how you spend your time

How can you do something to make your days less draining so you can have time to do the things you really want to do? To "Put Myself First" is all about learning tactics to utilize time efficiently so you have availability to do the things you want to do.

The following activities will give you a glimpse into how you spend your time and energy. Once you begin to take an honest look at your time, you can begin to take control of it, instead of it controlling you.

✂ **Activity: <u>Time Audit</u>**

Take a closer look at how you are currently spending your time. Use the below Time Audit Worksheet to log how you spend your time for three days. Choose one weekend day and two weekdays. Include the amount of time that you take to complete each activity, what the activity is, and how you feel when doing it. Whenever possible write down why you are doing something if it is not obvious. Try to list as many tasks as you can so it can help you determine where and when you are doing tasks that contribute to your overall well-being. Utilize extra paper if necessary.

Date	Time	Activity	Notes

At this point, you have spent three typical days tracking your time. Now take a moment to analyze your data.

What categories had many entries?

❑ Commuting	❑ Telephone calls	❑ Working on the computer
❑ Meetings	❑ Drop-In visitors	❑ Playing video games
❑ Paperwork	❑ Watching TV	❑ Eating / preparing food
❑ Reading	❑ Planning	❑ Other _____
❑ Relaxation	❑ Exercising	❑ Other _____

What were your time wasters?

❑ Fatigue	❑ Lack of planning	❑ Failure to delegate
❑ Travel	❑ Lack of priorities	❑ Meetings
❑ Poor filing	❑ Too much to do	❑ Lack of routines
❑ Phone calls	❑ Unexpected crisis	❑ Outside demands
❑ Interruptions	❑ Dis-organization	❑ Questionnaires
❑ Illness	❑ Procrastination	❑ People not available
❑ Paperwork	❑ Social distractions	❑ Other _____
❑ Junk mail	❑ Lack of resources	❑ Other _____

What activities did you do that you didn't need to do at all?

Why didn't you get everything accomplished?

What interruptions took you off schedule?

What did you learn from the time audit? *(Did you discover that you go about your daily routine without any thought to your activities? That you make decisions based upon habit or because someone else pressured you? That you have no method to manage your time - that someone else manages it for you?)*

How can you do something to make your days less draining so you can have fun?

✂ **Activity: <u>Daily Activity Wheel</u>**

Another way to look at how you spend a typical day is to fill out the Daily Activity Wheel. The daily activity wheel is a tool that will visually show you how you utilize your day by using a "pie chart." Consider each type of activity listed in the table below. Estimate how much time (in hours) you spend on each activity during an average day. Next, divide the estimated time by 24 to calculate what percentage of your day that activity is typically performed. Assign a color to represent each activity on the circle. Now transfer the information to the wheel. Beginning at the dot in the center of the circle, draw lines outward to depict the percentage of a day for each activity. Once you have accounted for each activity, color in the corresponding section of the chart. Then look at your completed activity wheel and see how you spend your time on a daily basis.

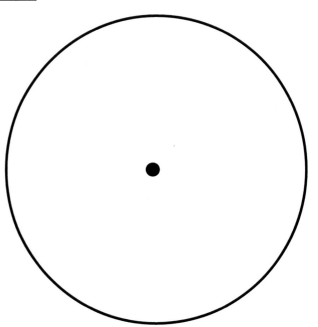

Activity	Description/Examples	Est. Time	%-24 hr. day	Color
Sleeping	Solid hours; if interrupted sleep use a dotted line			
Eating	Preparation and clean-up included			
Grooming	Hair, nails, makeup, etc.			
Exercising	Walking, yoga, swimming, weightlifting, etc.			
Working	Tasks, phone calls, e-mails, mtgs, paperwork			
Driving	Commuting, chauffeuring family			
Using electronics	TV, computer, cellphone, video games			
Spending time w/ children	Playing games, talking, reading, etc.			
Spend time with spouse	Loving, communicating, exploring, etc.			
Spend time with yourself	Meditation, prayer, and self-care			
Doing a hobby	Gardening, reading, knitting, etc.			
Housekeeping	Grocery shopping, maintenance, etc.			
Home administration	Paying bills, paperwork, etc.			
Structuring your dreams	Planning, achieving			

What did you learn from these exercises? Do you just go about your daily routine without any thought about the activities you do? Do you make your decisions based upon habit or because someone else pressures you into doing it? Did you realize you have no method of managing your time; therefore, it is managed for you?

✂ Activity: <u>Who Are You Living For Activity</u>

One issue that may have been uncovered in the above exercise is that other people rule how you expend energy. It is not uncommon to not be in control of your own time and as a result, are living for other people. Try the **Who Are You Living for Activity** to help you visualize if you are living for others rather than yourself.

In the first column, list things that you did for yourself this past week. These are not only things that develop your inner-self but also things that help you attain what is important in life. They are decisions that are made without the influence of anyone else. They can also be self-grooming tasks such as taking a bubble bath or flossing your teeth. These things might also be activities that you enjoy just for the sake of your enjoyment.

In the second column, list things that you did for other people. Examples may include writing a business document with your boss' name on it without acknowledging your authorship; attending a social gathering to mingle with the correct influential people; or taking out the trash for your child because he went to play soccer with his friends.

Yourself	Others

Which column is longer? If you are like most people, it is the "others" column. However, you will have to determine if sometimes the others' needs are important. Here are some examples to get you thinking. You may not have time to get a job and bring your family out of debt because you are too busy tending to your elderly mother. Or you may not have money to go to the dentist for yourself because you don't have enough to pay for the expensive car that your spouse purchased. Or, upon looking at the bills, they include video games and items that your children could live without.

Putting It All Into Action

Now that you have a better understanding of how you spend your time, you can start planning the activities that are most important in your life. You will plan each day before the day begins, preferably the night before. Before you begin, you will need to get the right tools in place.

✂ Tool: Daily Calendar

Many people are accustomed to using a month-at-a-glance calendar which can be a good tool to keep track of scheduled appointments such as doctor visits and family events. However, they usually do not have enough space for items associated with time periods. If you only use a monthly calendar, you are missing a vital last piece of your planning and organization. A daily calendar is important because its purpose is to help you plan how your day will progress. If you do not plan your day, then others will plan it for you.

When choosing a calendar, find one that has the time written out with at least half-hour increments with approximately twelve hours' worth of spaces. I recommend one that also has space for writing Task Items on the same page. See the sample at the end of the chapter.

(✂ Daily Calendar, p. 128)

(✂ Daily Calendar, p. 128)

Finally, understand that this tool will be the master calendar to which all other notes and calendar appointments will be transferred. So the spaces need to be big enough for writing not only the description of the appointment but also the related pertinent information.

✂ Tool: All-Encompassing Planner

The task list, month-at-a-glance, daily calendar, and goal setting worksheets can all be combined into one tool, a planner. There are many different types of planners on the market and each one contains different sections. I find that for most people, planners are overwhelming. However, if you like the binding or some of the sections then it is ok to remove the sections that are not needed. For example, you may already have a place to store addresses and may not need to use the address book in the planner.

🖥 Electronic Considerations: <u>Electronic Calendar</u>

An electronic calendar can be a helpful alternative option because it can be viewed in different ways (day, week, or month). Therefore, the user will not be stuck transferring appointments from a paper month-at-a-glance to the daily calendar. Another great feature of the electronic calendar is that it can be a receptacle for information such as location, phone number, and notes related to the appointment. Although most phones have pre-loaded calendar applications there are some other considerations when selecting the proper calendar application. Instead of listing the current considerations here, it is advised to check updated technology at the time of reading this book.

🔖 Tactic: <u>Planning the Daily Schedule</u>

This section could have been titled "creating the daily schedule" or "Using the Daily Calendar" but it is really about "planning." So often, people enter appointments into their calendar and give it no further thought, but as you will see making entries in your calendar takes some thought and planning.

Do not plan so much or schedule so tightly that you do not have the flexibility to adjust your schedule for interruptions. This is a great way to miss deadlines, or for things to accidentally slip through the cracks.

One note to consider regarding scheduling is to make sure that you consider environmental conditions. For example, you may want to schedule something fun like surfing, then consider when the waves and weather will be good. You will also need to schedule time for prerequisites such as putting on proper clothing and preparing a surfboard.

Schedule the rushing, menial chores when you typically have more energy but do not feel like thinking. Schedule the thinking projects when you are most alert. Schedule some activities at non-peak hours. You can do the activity at a slower pace and, hopefully, enjoy it more.

Don't be afraid to alter your schedule throughout a day based on unexpected events, when new responsibilities present themselves or your energy level changes. If you have time blocked off on your schedule to complete a project on the computer and the power goes out, instead of being stressed that you are not on schedule, take the opportunity to enjoy the quiet, catch up on reading, or practice meditation techniques.

Now that you have the correct tool and have a basic understanding of its use, you need to learn to use it properly. The following steps are designed to help you systematize your thought process of scheduling so you can better plan your day.

1. **Block off daily routines.**

Daily routines are often standard activities that occur at roughly the same time each day. People often forget to block off time in their schedule for them. Below are some examples of daily routines.

- Lunch preparation
- Preparing clothes for work/school
- Getting kids ready for school
- Housework
- Traveling to/from work
- Answering e-mail
- Returning phone calls
- Home paperwork
- Exercise
- Planning for the next day

In the *Attain Equilibrium* chapter, routines will be addressed in great detail.

2. **Block off time for routine tasks.**

In the *Slow Down* Chapter, you categorized like tasks such as bill paying and making a menu for the week. This is where you need to decide whether you want to consider these routine tasks as scheduled or unscheduled events. Some of them like phone calls may be unscheduled and others like bill paying may be scheduled. The criteria you should use is whether you will continually put it off if you do not set time aside for it or they occur regularly. Whether these routine tasks remain on the task list or become part of a scheduled time frame on the calendar, you would still file the associated paperwork in one of the task folders and mark the location of the paper in "( )" on either the task list or the calendar.

3. **Enter scheduled appointments (including drive time).**

When adding items to your calendar, first add items that have a set time associated with them, such as a doctor appointment or meeting. These may include standing appointments such as basketball practice or music lessons. If you also have a month-at-a-glance calendar, during this portion of planning each day, also transfer any appointments from the month-at-a-glance calendar to the daily schedule.

Part of an appointment is traveling to the location of the appointment. Make sure that travel time is noted in the appropriate spaces on the schedule. Always plan more time than needed to allow for potential delays along the route. Arriving at a destination early is not a bad thing. The additional time can be used to collect thoughts so the appointment can begin with a calm demeanor.

4. **Schedule Transition Time.**

Transition time is the time it takes to move from one activity to the next. For example, if you are working on something at home and need to get in the car to go to a meeting, you will need time to grab your keys, coat, and potentially paperwork or items needed for the meeting. You will also need time to get something to drink and go to the bathroom. Give yourself at least ten minutes.

5. **Schedule time for relaxing and spontaneity.**

There are two types of individuals regarding time utilization: those who plan and those who don't. Both types of people are presumably reading this book. For those of you who are already planners, then this is in here to remind you to make time to schedule fun and resting into your calendar. For those of you who are by nature not planners, this section of the book is here to help you learn how to plan so you can get things accomplished but remain free-spirited.

You really may need to write Spontaneity onto your calendar so you don't forget to lighten up and have fun. My father used to joke about it with his friends. Sorry, Dad, this is no joking matter.

6. **Scheduling unscheduled time.**

The remaining unscheduled time is for accomplishing tasks or projects. This portion of the plan only looks at finding the time to work on your task list, not actually doing them. For example, if you are organizing your kitchen cabinets today, schedule at least a two-hour time block to work on it. Do not try to squeeze it in when you are not doing something else. The *Prioritize* chapter will show how to estimate the time it takes to accomplish tasks, as well as prioritize and sequence the task list.

See the **Daily Calendar Example** (✂ p. 129) for an idea of how the calendar should be filled in. In the sample, notice routines such as meals and prep time are blocked off.

📌 Tactic: <u>Scheduling Each Week</u>

It is also important to look at your whole week at a glance. This is helpful when deciding what days you have available to accomplish larger projects that may require concentration and follow-through. For example, you may not want to start a project such as sewing curtains for the whole house on a day when you have to go to a doctor's appointment right before lunchtime. Instead, you would save that project for a day that you do not have commitments in the middle of the day. This will allow time to break at a reasonable point instead of having to cut the activity short to make it to your appointment on time.

The time to plan your week can be at the end of the previous week (Friday afternoon) or it can be at the beginning of the week (Sunday night). When you are planning your week, you would make sure any tasks are listed on the corresponding daily calendar.

One time I was driving home from an activity with my son and was rushing because I was meeting someone at the house. My son did not care that we were going to be cutting it close to the designated time. I reminded him of the rule learned by his older sister in the high school band. If you are 15 minutes early then you are on time. If you are on time then you are late. If you are late, then don't bother showing up.

His reply: "Since we are already going to be late, can we go for ice cream?"

♀ Taking it Deeper

✂ Tactic: <u>Putting myself first at work</u>

Do what you were born to do. Period. Before reading any further remember: the most important part of work is to be in a profession that you enjoy. If you are not having fun at your job you will always feel like it is work. If you are not in a job that you enjoy, take the time to explore your interests and skills to determine another field that may be better suited for you.

I know it is easier said than done. Even if you are not in your dream job, you still need to put yourself first. Business today is more demanding than ever.

- **Read the employee handbook.**

  The only way for a business organization to survive and for you to remain with it is to know the mission of the business and how you fit into it. Even if it is long, take the time to read it. A good understanding of what is expected of you and other employees is the basic step to doing the right things with little wasted effort and lots of enjoyment.

- **Read the company's marketing collateral.**

  It portrays a message and gives a good understanding of the reason for the business. What keeps the company going? What brings in the money? If you cannot understand these things by reading, ask a senior manager or personnel associate to explain them to you. This will help you strengthen your sense of personal purpose within the confines of the company.

- **Re-read your position description.**

  Having a defined position description will show how you fit in to the company. If you do not have one, make one. Ask your boss to assist you with this project, because it is very important to know what you are supposed to be doing. When faced with choices about how to spend our time, understanding what you are supposed to be doing will help you make decisions about what to do.

- **Make your own mission statement for your little niche within the company.** The corporate goals/duties should assist a person in recognizing and achieving their own mission and goals.

- **Review/write yearly or quarterly goals.** If your company does not already have a process of personal goal setting, write your own. Even if they are not within the confines of your current job description, you can seek to achieve goals that will help you where you want to go as a person. For example, if you have always loved making presentations but work in manufacturing, find ways to integrate presentations into your current job even if you have to work overtime or on your own time to accomplish it. Learn how to do your job more efficiently so you can squeeze in extra tasks that you like to do. Look at where you want to go and set the goals to get there.

"Who are We?" Book Five in the Ringing Cedars Series
by Vladimir Merge

... say a Man lives eighty years...Clothing, housing, and food are provided for him by his parents. But the parents also attempt, either consciously or subconsciously, through their behavior, to impart to him their thoughts and the way they see the world around them. The visible process of getting to know what life is all about lasts approximately eighteen years. .. Over the remaining sixty-two years of his life, ... let us try to calculate how much time he is free to think for himself.... If you multiply ... eight hours per day (by 62 years of Man's life as a basis)..., you find that Man sleeps for 587,928 hours of his life. Thus sleeping 8 hours a day equates to 22 years of constant sleep. Now subtract 22 years from 62 years of his life and we have 40 years when he is awake.

...Preparation and consumption of food every day comes to ... 7 years. Subtract this number from the 40 and there are 33 left.

...Spend each day on work... eight hours with another two or so spend getting to and from work...for the thirty years of so-call work activity he spends ten years constantly working for someone... And now from those 33 years of life we have to subtract another 10, leaving us 23.

...watches TV... three hours per day... 8 years of constant sitting in front of a television screen. If we take them away from the 23 remaining, we are left with 15. But even this time is not free for activities native to Man alone. It cannot make a sudden switch from one thing to another. Some time is spent processing and making sense of the information received. All told, the average Man spends only 15 to 20 minutes of his life reflecting on the mystery of creation.

(Merge, 2001) Paraphrased from the section "Do we have freedom of thought?"

Many times, I have contemplated that chapter from Vladimir Merge's book which reminds the reader to look at time utilization over the entire life instead of on a day to day basis. However, the daily choices are the ones that will dictate the usage of time over the long haul. If you want to put yourself first, you need to commit your actions to new habits. You can spend a lifetime "un-learning" your habit of living for others or you can spend thousands of dollars talking to a professional about your reasons for (...) – you fill in the blank. I intend to point out some of the common barriers to putting yourself first. However, if any of these or other barriers are an individual issue, please find a life coach or read further on the topic.

- **Unclear priorities are one of the most common barriers to putting yourself first.** You do not know what you want to do, so you just do the things that are put in front of you. In a previous chapter, you wrote down your mission statement and the top three beliefs. After writing them down, if you still have not started living them, then examine why.

- **You may be experiencing perfectionism.** Perfectionists are afraid to make a mistake because they do not want to admit that they have limitations. They do not want others to know they are human. They want to be super-human or they do not want to be let down or let someone else down. "If I don't even try, I can't fail," is the secret mantra of a perfectionist. You do not have to be perfect to live your life; you are the only one who is living it. Do not be afraid to live your beliefs.

- **Another scenario may be the global thinker who tries to do many ambitious projects all at once and jams progress.** The **Action Planning Worksheet (p. 43)** is a good tool for people with this tendency.

- **Another barrier to not putting yourself first could be a lack of assertiveness.** You may not know how to say "no" when asked to do something for fear that you might disappoint or even anger the other person. Or you may not assert your own wishes for fear that you are imposing on the other person. Being assertive is not the same as being aggressive. Asserting yourself is letting others know what you want, and at the same time, not forcing others to do what you want. The Abilene paradox states that a group of people collectively decide on a course of action that is counter to the preferences of many or all of the individuals in the group. Doing things with others is most often the common ground of all parties wanting to do something together and sometimes requires assertiveness.

- **Another obstacle could be the inability to make decisions.** Just like in a group, sometimes lack of forethought causes individuals to perform actions that are counter to their personal preferences.

📌 Tactic: <u>Living Consistently Within Your Core</u>

There will be many times where your core beliefs will be challenged. People will try to manipulate you into doing what they want or try to mold you to fit in with their own core beliefs. Some people have no trouble sticking to their beliefs while others need a little reminder. Use the **About Me Worksheet** (✂ **Activity** p. 78) in the *Slow Down* Chapter as a creed to yourself that you can carry with you to remind yourself what you stand for and believe in. Whenever you feel pressed for time, look at your About Me Worksheet to make better decisions concerning time.

Do not waste your time on people or activities that do not fit into your core values. For example, if one of your core values is to honor Mother Earth, then you may choose an Earth Day celebration over a bachelor party of a work acquaintance.

Here are some ways that you can re-affirm your commitment to living consistently within your core:

- **Schedule time alone**. There is no correct answer as to how much time you should spend alone. However, the absolute minimum should be 30 minutes daily. If you are only taking 30 minutes then you should use it as a total quiet time where you do not "do" anything but just sit or lie down and let your mind rest. If you have more than 30 minutes, then use the time to go with the flow of what tasks come naturally. This could be a time where you will not try to accomplish your "task" list but instead, just do things that you enjoy doing.
- **Incorporate your mission into your daily life.** Spend time each day doing something that fits with your mission of who you are. If you are consistent with spending at least 15 minutes each day, then after about a month you will begin to see that you are living

consistently within your core. Consider the fable of the hare and the tortoise who are having a race. The hare knows he is faster than the tortoise so he thinks that he will win with no problem. He zips off and is very close to the finish line and decides to do other things and eventually falls asleep. While he is sleeping the tortoise creeps past him and passes the finish line. Slow and steady always wins.

- **Set a Personal Development Commitment**. Each year on your birthday or another annual reminder such as New Year's Day, take time to evaluate what you want to accomplish or learn for the year. **Choose only one**. Since many other things in life will come your way, you will not be able to focus on more. This is different than your goals. This is something you will focus on in your free time. It does not have to mean anything to anyone other than you. It should be something which gives you pleasure. For example, one year you may choose to learn a musical instrument or learn to paint. Another year you may focus on making your home a sanctuary for renewal and peace of mind. And another year you many commit to cleaning out all the clutter in your home. Write down your personal commitment which can be used throughout the year as a reminder to yourself.

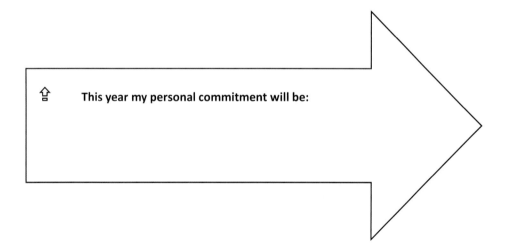

This year my personal commitment will be:

🖈 Tactic: <u>Honoring Yourself and Your Environment</u>

To truly put yourself first you need to honor yourself every day. When planning your day, make good choices. Start with good choices for your physical body. Go to bed by 10 pm. Sleep well. Wake up by 6 am. Shower daily. Stay hydrated. Eat well and promote nutrient absorption and good digestion. Exercise and maintain a healthy weight.

Honor the physical environment in which you live. If you don't have enough time to care for your environment, then you are doing too much. You will learn more about handling the overabundance of items in the *Lighten your Load* Chapter but start with the spaces you use every day such as your kitchen and bathroom.

You may be wondering, "How do I have time for making my way in the world if I am already spending so much time on physical self and environment?" Work some of these self-care tasks into your day. For example, take the stairs. They may take more time, but less time than if you have to drive to the gym, change, shower afterward, and then drive home.

If you do make one poor choice, don't let yourself spiral and continually make poor choices. It is the good choices over your lifetime that matter. If you have already done the damage, do what you can to keep it at bay. It will take discipline and determination.

One year I took scheduling to the next level and worked health considerations from Traditional Chinese Medicine and Ayurveda into a routine schedule. See below example:

Before Breakfast	2 cups of warm water (optional to add juice of ¼ lime)
	Oil body (at least feet)
	Exercise (Brisk walk, tai chi, meditation, yoga, etc.)
Breakfast	1 fruit (raw-summertime; dry/ soaked- wintertime)
	2 vegetable servings
	Handful of nuts (soaked)
	If extra hungry- extra protein
8-12am :	Mental Powers/ Work/ Accomplish Tasks
	Drink herbal tea
Lunch-Main Meal	2 servings of veggies (including roots and leaves)
	Animal protein (if at all for day)
	Best time for salad
	Only time for yogurt and other fermented foods
	No fruit
1-5pm :	Solve Problems and Get Organized
Afternoon Snack and Tea	Herbal tea/ fruits and nuts (soaked)
Dinner	Cooked leafy greens (1 serving)
	2 vegetable serving
	If extra hungry, 1 non animal protein
	No starchy foods at night
6-8pm :	Socialize
8-9pm :	Meditate and Relax
9pm- 5am :	Sleep

⊕ Quick Hits

- Keep a journal. A journal is a place where you can write down what you are thinking and feeling. It is a place for you to make sense of the world without outside influences. A journal does not have to be fancy, a spiral-bound notebook is less expensive.
- Take time out for rest.
- Practice spirituality. Spirituality is a time to rejuvenate the spirit. Spirituality is different for everyone. Some may go to church or synagogue regularly while others religiously practice a martial art.
- Practice saying "No."
- Live life like it is a vacation.

Daily Calendar

*Day & Date*_____

Schedule	
5:00 am	
5:30 am	
6:00 am	
6:30 am	
7:00 am	
7:30 am	
8:00 am	
8:30 am	
9:00 am	
9:30 am	
10:00 am	
10:30 am	
11:00 am	
11:30 am	
12:00 pm	
12:30 pm	
1:00 pm	
1:30 pm	
2:00 pm	
2:30 pm	
3:00 pm	
3:30 pm	
4:00 pm	
4:30 pm	
5:00 pm	
5:30 pm	
6:00 pm	
6:30 pm	
7:00 pm	
7:30 pm	
8:00 pm	
8:30 pm	

✓	Tasks	Priority

Daily Calendar Example

Day & Date _____

Schedule		✓	Tasks	Priority
5:00 am	Exercise		Call about electric bill	A
5:30 am			Enter phone # into	A
6:00 am	Shower/bathing		Schedule appt w/Dr	B
6:30 am			Work on taxes	A
7:00 am	Breakfast		Call Mr. Jones	B
7:30 am			Write proposal	B
8:00 am	Drive to Dr's Appt		Laundry	
8:30 am	Dr's Appt		Order sweater	
9:00 am	Task List			
9:30 am				
10:00 am	Snack			
10:30 am	Task List			
11:00 am	Staff Meeting			
11:30 am				
12:00 pm	Lunch			
12:30 pm				
1:00 pm				
1:30 pm	Work on project			
2:00 pm				
2:30 pm				
3:00 pm				
3:30 pm				
4:00 pm	Errands			
4:30 pm				
5:00 pm				
5:30 pm	Dinner / Clean up			
6:00 pm				
6:30 pm	Plan For Tomorrow			
7:00 pm	Fun Time			
7:30 pm				

Chapter 7: Phase 2- 🕸 Prioritize

This phase, which includes the strategy Live in the Present, brings everything covered thus far together. It shows you how to use a task list with the task drawer and how to prioritize tasks in conjunction with what is happening each day. It will set you up for success when you get down to the actual doing, the micro organization.

In the *Slow Down* Chapter, it was suggested that you take the time to write down all your tasks and file all of the items needed to complete the task. If you have not done this, do it now!

In the *Put Myself First* chapter, you presumably created your daily schedule. If you have not done this, do it now! Now you need to decide what tasks to complete during the unscheduled time in your calendar.

You previously used a task list entitled "Tasks - Now" which was used as a temporary place to capture tasks that needed immediate attention. This was a way to help you not lose sight of the tasks that needed to be done during the transition. This chapter will focus on transitioning away from using the temporary list to utilizing a more permanent one. To choose which option would work for you, you will need to decide whether to follow this process on a daily basis or a weekly one. The determining factor on whether to choose the **Weekly Task List** (✂ **p 55**) or the task list associated with the **Daily Calendar** (✂ **p 128**) is the number of tasks that you are required to complete. The daily option would be better for working professionals who also have many home and child-related tasks. Weekly Task List is sufficient for other individuals who have fewer overall tasks to accomplish.

With both of these options, at least one month's worth of task lists should be on hand. Many products on the market provide one year's worth of pages. If you are using the sheets provided in this book, you will need to make photocopies and then write the appropriate dates on the top of the pages. Writing the dates on at least one month's worth of task lists will create a placeholder for logging tasks.

For tasks whose start date extends past the prepared pages, you can choose to use the **Tasks – Future** (✂) or create one in a different format such as **Future Task List.** Take a look at each format to determine which one would work for you.

Regardless of which options are chosen, the steps are the same.

Future Tasks

Year _____

January	July
February	August
March	September
April	October
May	November
June	December

🖈 Tactic: Update the Task List

Take out the list entitled Tasks - Now and integrate the tasks from that list into a new routine process that follows. Remember that any item associated with a task should reference the location of the item.

1. **Review tasks already on the list.**

   Evaluate all the tasks listed to determine if and when they need to be started. Ask yourself questions such as the following. Does this task need to be done today/this week? Does it need to be done, ever?

   Note: At this point, you are only making decisions about **IF** and **WHEN** something has to be done. You are not spending mental and emotional energy on the specifics. In other words, don't get distracted doing the tasks now.

2. **Transfer priority tasks to the current task list.**

   Start using your preferred task list, and transfer the remaining tasks from the "Now" list onto the selected "permanent" task lists. On the "Now" list, write an arrow (->) in the left-most column of the task list to signify that task has been moved.

3. **Transfer non-priority tasks to "future" lists.**

   As you begin filling up your current list you may realize that all these tasks may not be able to be accomplished during the current day or week. If you are certain that a task needs to be put off, rewrite the task onto the Task List for the date/week that you think you will work on the task. On the "Now" list, write an arrow (->) in the left-most column of the task list to signify that task has been moved. If the estimated completion date is for a time period not within the boundaries of your current calendar or task book, then write it onto the Future Task List.

   NOTE: It will be important to allow time in your week to reassign items to and from your weekly and/or monthly calendar, future "task" list, and daily schedule. Although it may seem tedious, it will prevent worry about something that has to be done in the future so you can spend your time working confidently in the present.

One of the common questions people ask is: How do I know on what date to write a task? Sometimes you cannot estimate the exact day or even week, you just know it does not have to be done today. Randomly select a day, week, or month when you anticipate you will have time or it needs to be completed. When the time arrives, you can decide then if it needs to be done that day or not. If not, you will follow the above process to reassign the task to another day. Do not be concerned that tasks are being put off. However, if you habitually procrastinate, then you need to re-visit the prior chapters and take each phase more slowly.

Also, you should plan each day realistically to not overcrowd the schedule. Remember that everyone needs time in their day for rest and relaxation. You are no exception. Assign yourself fewer tasks so you can get in the habit of completing them.

🖥 Electronic Considerations: <u>Electronic Task List Dates</u>

If you are using an electronic task list, it is easy to add an entry without a date. So extra care should be given to assigning dates. Make a rule for yourself.

⇧ Do not add something to the electronic task list without assigning it a date.

⚑ Tactic: Prioritize and Sequence Tasks

Simply knowing all the items on the task list will not be sufficient. It will be essential to assign some sort of order of importance to them. Prioritizing will allow you to *deliberately* choose your actions and focus your energy on important activities.

Before you begin learning to prioritize, remember this: we reap what we sow. In other words, we get results where we put our energy. Before you learn the next tactic, take a minute to think about time in relation to yourself. The quote from the Ringing Cedars Series book in the *Put Myself First* Chapter should have gotten you thinking about how you spend your time but also consider the way the movie *In Time* helps clarify how to prioritize your day.

The movie *In Time* takes place in a future where the currency is time. People in the movie spend time working to pay for things such as a home, or electric bill, or food. From the viewpoint of the movie, it is easier to make decisions on how to spend time. For example, one hour of work is towards the next meal at a restaurant or it can be used to purchase food for the next five days. However, the purchased food requires five hours to prepare meals leaving five fewer hours available to work. In other words, each block of time spent can be viewed in terms of what it will gain. Will it eat away at the available time with no purpose or will it help sustain life?

On a more personal level, when setting priorities there are two different kinds to consider: tasks that need to be done for "day-to-day" life, and tasks that are goal-related. Look back at the TIME AUDIT you completed earlier in the *Put Myself First* chapter. Did it include any of the items that are most important to you? Did you spend your time completing fruitless tasks? When thinking about what you need to accomplish, you need to balance both types of priorities. *If you are always doing routine tasks only, you will never feel like you get anything significant accomplished. If you only work on bigger picture items, then you will get stressed from all the undone tasks.*

Keep this in mind as you plan your upcoming week. You should plan your week around your most important priorities that could be related to your personal goals, yet allow time for completing day-to-day and routine tasks.

Planning your week around your most important priorities might be completely foreign to you. However, start with taking fifteen minutes a day to do something important to you. After a month of being consistent with the fifteen minutes, I suspect that you will already start shifting your daily priorities to allow the time necessary to truly start to balance tasks that are goal-related versus those that are "day-to-day" life and routine tasks.

Sometimes, you need to complete all of the annoying trivia or distractions that can't be put off first before concentrating on the big important goal. This will help give you a sense of accomplishment and is okay as long as it is not a procrastination tool. However, I contend that once you start making future "task" lists and clear your mind of all the possible tasks that pop through your head, you will be less inclined to have to complete all of the little things first because your mind will trust that you have a system in place to remember them when the time is right.

Therefore, when planning a day or weeks' worth of potential tasks, your list contains both routine tasks and bigger picture items.

To carve out larger chunks of time for projects that cannot be broken up or that may need to be uninterrupted, schedule time on the calendar as if it was an appointment. You are in essence scheduling an appointment with yourself. For example, you would want to schedule uninterrupted time to make curtains for your house. If you get interrupted it is very hard to leave them half pinned. However, be wary of scheduling too much time for these appointments that you delay completing the smaller tasks to a point where their incompletion becomes problematic. If you wanted to make curtains for several rooms, for example, you may have to plan to make one a month so you can still have time to work on daily tasks such as food preparation and cleaning.

Try breaking the prioritization process down into the following steps.

1. **Identify the most important reminder of the day/week.**

When planning your week, use the "**Remember to:**" box on the **Weekly Task List** (χ p. 55) to write down the one major thing you want to accomplish this week. For example, I often get so wrapped up in working that I forget to take breaks so a common entry on my list is "Get Outside."

2. **Assign each Task an "A" or "B" Priority.**

The next step to putting your plan into action is deciding the importance of getting a task done. Take a look at all of the entries on the list and write an "A" or a "B" in the priority column.

- An "A" priority is an activity that must be done today or tomorrow or if you are using the Weekly Task List, this week. It will become a crisis because of the incomplete task. Or an "A" priority can be an activity that is related to your goals or core values.
- A "B" priority is important, but not necessarily urgent.

In setting A or B priority, use the following questions to help you make decisions:

- Which is most important?
- Which activities contribute to my purpose?
- Which yields the greatest benefit for my time?

- Which reinforces my values?
- What can I delegate?
- What can I do more quickly?
- If I could do only one activity today, which would it be?
- Does it directly support a role I play such as a parent, employee, child, etc.?
- Which ones are alike and can be done together (i.e. phone calls)?
- Will it make me more knowledgeable and help me fulfill my potential?
- Is it important to someone I care about?
- Will it matter a year from now?
- What can I postpone?
- What can I get out of?
- What are the consequences if I do not complete each activity today?
- Does it have a deadline set by someone else?
- Is it an order from someone (supervisor, parent, spouse) whom I cannot ignore?
- Will it matter if I do not do it at all?

3. **Sequence the Tasks.**
   - After you have an "A" or a "B" written next to each task, sequence the A's in numerical order. Number one would be the task to be done first, two is the second, and so on. Sometimes A1 is the closest to fulfilling your purpose or goal and sometimes it is the most urgent.
   - Next, Sequence the B's in a similar manner starting with the number one again.

Note: Using this method, the tasks do not need to be written in the order that they are to be completed. By looking at your prioritized list, you will know what to do and in what order. Thus when working on tasks the eye can find A1, A2, A3, then B1, B2, and so on.

✦ Tactic: Sequence Tasks for Projects

When you have papers on which there are multiple related tasks, you should use the

Action Planning Worksheet (✂ p. 43).

1. **Add Tasks As Necessary.**

   Consider, AT THE SAME TIME, all of the tasks that need to be completed for the project, meeting, or group of related tasks and add as needed.

2. **Sequence the Tasks.**

   After listing all of the tasks on the worksheet as described in the *Simplify Your Life* Chapter, write numbers in the sequence column to denote the order that the tasks should be accomplished. Sometimes it may be tricky to determine the exact sequence. The first few and the last few might be apparent but the middle may be unclear. In some cases such as that, just randomly assign the sequence. For example, if you were holding a yard sale it might be easy to determine the first tasks of setting a date, and advertising as well as last tasks such as gathering change and pricing. However, some of the tasks in the middle such as finding display tables or gathering items to sell could be done in any order.

   Note: The tasks do not have to be written on the sheet in the order that you intend to do them.

3. **Assign Due Dates.**

   Once the sequence is assigned to each entry, start and/or due dates can be determined for each of the items. When considering dates at the overall project level, it is easier to be realistic.

4. **Transfer each distinct task from the Project Planning Worksheet to the appropriate current or future task list for completion.** If there are any materials needed to complete the task, do not forget to note their location in parentheses and file the materials in the proper WIP areas.

5. **File or trash the Project Planning Worksheet without worry that you will forget to do something on it.** It will already be on your list, ready to remind you when the day comes.

Chapter 8 - 🕸 Living in the Present

The past is what shaped us into what we are today but we should not dwell on all the mistakes we have made. We are the sum total of our experiences. We shouldn't say "If only I…" or "What if I…?" Once you change your thinking on this, life becomes easy. It makes letting go of possessions easier. It helps the decision-making process and allows change to enter your life.

One of the reasons that people get stuck and don't consider major changes is because they get comfortable in their ways. If you break your arm, moving through your daily tasks could be different. So you change your habit and start microwaving prepared food. When the arm heals, you continue purchasing prepared food and using the microwave to do the simplest of kitchen warming such as warming water for tea. You may have created the habits subconsciously during a time when you needed them, but then you continued those habits. Living in the present is about consciously shifting your daily habits to be more in line with your core values. As you start to put in new practices, I challenge you to create habits based on conscious choices.

Putting It All Into Action:

📌 Tactic: Using the Task List

Start at A1 and continue working on tasks.

1. **Check completed tasks.**

   Once a task is completed, in pencil, place a checkmark (✓) in the ✓ column or the "completed" column depending upon which task list was selected.

Note: Some people may prefer to use color to track finished tasks. I do not recommend this because having extra colors on the page is more distracting. Although it may not be thrilling to check off an item on a list, in the long run, it will be less disruptive and help focus attention appropriately. However, if adding color makes it more game-like and will help you get through the list more effectively, then use color.

2. **Notate Open Tasks.**

   If a task is started but it is not completed and you subsequently work on a different task, place an "O" in front of it. "O" stands for Open. By doing this, when you leave the list and later come back to it, your eye can be more quickly drawn to the entry on which the open task is not completed.

3. **Check Previously Open Tasks.**

   When you ultimately complete it, place a check (✓) inside the "O" to denote completion.

4. **Bring Closure to The Current Task List.**

   At the end of the day, there will invariably be items that do not have a ✓ or and an X next to them. The last task before turning to a new list is to bring closure to the current list.

   - **Carry forward every open item on your task list.** If you are using a paper system, re-write the task on the appropriate day/week list. If there are tasks that need to be completed within a future time frame, use the selected Future Task List as a placeholder for these entries.

   - **On the current list, put an arrow (→) next to the task signifying that it has been moved.**

   - **For tasks that are no longer relevant, place an "X" in the ✓ column of the list.** For example, if you had on the list to schedule a service worker but ended up doing the chore yourself, you would no longer need to schedule the service worker. Thus an "X" would be an appropriate notation to signify closure to that task.

   Before transitioning to the next list, every item should have a ✓, x, or →next to it. In the past, I have gone so far as to lightly write a ✓ on the entire page thus signifying a completed list. By consciously going through this process, you never have to worry about if you forget to complete a task. This routine is part of a larger routine to help you remain organized. The entire routine will be covered in the *Attain Equilibrium* chapter.

🖥 Electronic Considerations: <u>Clearing the Electronic Task List.</u>

Many electronic task systems change the color of past due tasks. Thus, at the end of the day, it is easy to change the date of the uncompleted task.

📌 Tactic: <u>Integrating Backlog into the task list</u>

As mentioned in the *Slow Down* chapter, schedule chunks of time to whittle down the already existing piles of paper and clutter. If there are smaller tasks that arise from your scheduled sessions, then create individual entries on your task list for them. Here are some examples of backlog items that can be integrated into the new routine.

- **Piece of paper on which a note was written to call the lawyer about updating the Will.** This is not totally urgent but very important, so it can go on a list in the next month. Once you transpose the information to the list, the scrap of paper can be discarded.

- **Paper from the state about a disabled relative that should have been filled out last year.** Someone is not beating down the door to get the paper but it really should be addressed. Write it on the list, note the location of the paper in parentheses and file the paper in the Task Drawer.

- **Packet of seeds that a friend gave two years ago.** Although the seeds may be outdated, they may still grow so go ahead and sprinkle them on the ground. If you are not doing it today, then write a note on the day/week you are going to do it and put the packet of seeds in the appropriate staging area.

- **Matchbook from a restaurant where you enjoyed a show and want to go see another show.** Write the name and website or phone number of the place on the task list (for whatever month you may want to go again), then integrate the matches into the zone for matches.

In the *Stabilize* chapter you filled out a **Needs Assessment – HOME** (✂ p. 100) that was designed to help you take a critical look at the clutter within certain zones. The "No" answers on this assessment could be considered backlog. Now that you have an understanding of the planning process, you can add to your list individual tasks that were previously identified as one task labeled: "create schedule of organizing (O)." Pull the corresponding sheet out of the "O" task drawer.

Do you still agree with the assessment you gave to yourself at that time? Were there any areas that arose since then that need to be added to the priorities from the Needs Assessment? If yes, add that area to the bottom of the Needs Assessment list. Now look at all the "No" answers on your needs assessment and any handwritten areas and add them to the appropriate task list.

📌 Tactic: No Multi-tasking

Part of living in the present is doing only one thing at a time. In other words, no multi-tasking. Multitasking is giving mental energy to more than one thing at a time. For example, do not try to answer e-mails while stirring sauce for dinner. However, if you have already prepared dinner and are waiting for it to cook in the oven, you may have time to empty the dishwasher.

Some guidelines for this concept are as follows:

⇧ Do not leave the room while working on a task if the task has to be monitored.

⇧ Interrupt a task only if it has a built-in wait period or you need a break.

⇧ Do not create an unnecessary wait period which the task does not intrinsically need.

⇪ Do not start many tasks but finish none of them.

⚲ Taking it Deeper

Do you wake up each day raring to go? Fully living in the present starts with a commitment to understanding your spirit. Spirit is the essence of what is inside you that makes you tick; it makes you who you are and fulfills you. Some synonyms for spirit are strength, character, and moral fiber. It can also be defined as one's sense of life or vitality. Often people equate spirit with religion. However, you do not have to be religious to explore your spirit.

Being able to recognize the things that make you truly happy is the first step to understanding your spirit. Go back to your **Personal Observation Questions** (✂ p. 31) and reflect upon what truly makes you happy and lifts your spirit. What is the common characteristic of the activities you enjoy? Are they outdoors? Are they using your artistic abilities? Are they exploring your beliefs? Below are some examples of activities that might be on a list of items that make you happy.

- Take a walk outside.
- Take your dog to play in the park.
- Play a musical instrument.
- Paint a picture.
- Go canoeing.
- Roll around in the grass with your favorite toddler.
- Build a fire in the fireplace and contemplate it.
- Chopping Walnuts. Ok seeing if you are paying attention, this is actually on my list.

When was the last time that you actually did one of those activities? Make a commitment to yourself to do at least one activity a day that lifts your spirit. You will only be able to work on lifting your spirit and vitality when you are not bogged down with all of the previously identified time-wasters such as watching television or working on the computer. This will not happen overnight. If you are reading this book in sequential order, by the time you get to the *Attain Equilibrium* chapter, you truly should be able to work on your spirit.

📌 Tactic: <u>Transitioning</u>

Many times people are unorganized and do not live in the present because they have not learned how to transition out of one situation into another. Their mind is still on the activity that they did not close out and they cannot fully function in the present activity until they catch up. The solution is very obvious. Schedule transition time into your day to put closure to one activity before moving on to the next. If you are concerned that you will transition more quickly than anticipated and will get to the next activity too soon, good. Being early will assure that you will be mentally prepared for the new activity.

Physically transitioning items from one place to another is another concern. One of the ways I have continued to stay organized and live in the present is to utilize what I call **"The Lunchbox System."** Since I am always taking food with me when I go places, I carry a lunch box. When I need to bring items to and from places, I put them into my lunchbox so I don't forget them. Then when I get to my destination, I empty the entire lunch box, take out the items that are needed for that activity, and put the lunch back in. At the end of the day, after I return home, I empty the entire lunch box again, handle what is in it, including cleaning dirty dishes, and I am ready for the next day. You can use this system with any type of bag that you carry to and from your home every day, it does not have to be a lunchbox.

🔖 Tactic: <u>Getting Closure</u>

As I was working with one client we realized that she is living in the present so much that she drops whatever she has been working on to give her attention to the latest and greatest "whatever."

Therefore, nothing is ever fully closed out and as a result, she has MANY unresolved tasks. We have created the task list and the task filing system but she never looks at it without me. As we tried to uncover why, we decided that there was something scary about closure. By leaving the tasks incomplete, she could go back to that portion of her life.

Well, you are never going to be where you were. The incomplete tasks will continue to accumulate and compound. In other words, the backlog will grow. So make a commitment to whittle away at them.

🔖 Tactic: <u>Be</u>

We are conditioned to the way of "doing." Did you ever get so wrapped up in your world and the things you have to do that you cannot remember something as simple as your address or mother's first name? You may be so busy doing things and thinking about what you are doing next that you forget who you are. The assumption is if you are not doing something then there is something wrong with you. This idea comes from the foundation of the United States, especially in New England, of a Puritan work ethic to be productive and responsible. Also, in a capitalist society, if we are not productive, we are not contributing to the good of the community or nation. We are afraid of losing control. If we slowed down to a more balanced pace and took time to enjoy life, what might happen? Would nothing get done? Would anything get done? Would we survive? Frightened of loosening our grip, we struggle to impose our agenda on life instead of going with the flow of being.

The opposite of "doing" is "being." It is one of the lessons taught in Buddhism that many Westerners have a hard time understanding. "Being" is the pause between thoughts or the space in which everything comes and goes.

In Zen, the corresponding approach to meditation is called "just sitting." In everyday life, it takes the form of "just walking," "just eating," or "just driving." In other words, total absorption in every activity without separation. Live in the present, effortlessly!

Try to live in the present along your journey. Whenever you go to a place where you have to wait, just sit and observe. Did you ever notice how children have no trouble talking to strangers in waiting rooms? They are being themselves and sharing their gifts.

📌 Tactic: <u>Let Go of the Past</u>

Living in the present means to let go of the things: painful experiences, traumatic incidents, losses, irreversible mistakes, regrettable decisions, from your past that are holding you down. This is the part of the journey that only you can do. It requires going even deeper and takes a lot of effort. Find a therapist, a support group, an alternative medicine practitioner, or a good energy worker such as a chakra healer, voice healer, Reiki practitioner, massage therapist, or flower essence practitioner. Find someone who is trained to help you unlock your potential and get rid of the blocks in your energy system.

⏱ Quick Hits

- **Don't waste energy on things that will already happen.** If you can determine that forces in play will already make something happen, why worry about it? A personal example that I have used in the past is the following. I was going to a conference and someone asked questions such as "Where was it?", "When is it going to start?" I replied that I didn't know. Since it was only a week away, they looked at me strangely. My response was, "When it is time for me to know, I will know." In other words, I wasn't wasting energy on it because it was going to happen, and I would find out the details as time got closer.

- **Create a "perhaps" list** to write down things that you might want to do someday. Writing a list can help take away the feeling that you have to constantly remember things.

- **Schedule things at non-peak hours.** For example, leave for work slightly after rush hour or go grocery shopping in the early morning when others are sleeping.

- **Live in the present by listening to your body.** Sleep when you are tired and eat when you are hungry.

- **Give yourself more time between tasks** to process and finish the job.

- **Plan and pace efforts.** For example, if you like to read, then read one book a month, that is twelve per year. Which twelve will they be? How will you spend that time?

Keep in mind these tips about using the task list:

You do not have to complete your entire list in one day. Although a part of you may be screaming, but...I must I MUST because I know tomorrow an even larger list awaits me, ignore it. As long as you are alive, you will never have a blank list. Get over having to feel like you must complete it.

Don't worry about taking items off the list. When you add a potential task to a future day's list, you may think it is very important. However, when that day comes you may realize that you were unrealistic in adding it in the first place. For example, a client was going away in April and did not complete his taxes which were due by April 15. Before he left, he gathered all of the necessary items needed and asked me to mail them to his accountant. The day after he left, he left me a message stating that if there was an issue, have the accountant file an extension and they can deal with it when he returns. I sent the package with the note about the extension to the accountant. Furthermore, I sent the accountant an e-mail that the package would be coming and she replied. About a week later, I put on my list to call her to see if there were any problems with it. After putting the task off for two days, I finally took it off my list. Why should I worry about whether my client's accountant had any issues with his taxes? He would get a call if there were.

Do not worry about finishing a task on the same day it was started. Although you may want closure with every task you have on your list, you cannot. For example, you may need to contact someone about signing up for a class that you want to take at the local gym. You may have left a message and are awaiting a callback. The difference between this and the previous example is that this task is one that you initiated and is important to you. If you take it off the list and the other person does not call you back, you may forget.

Do some task related to your innermost purpose each day *at a time when you are most alert.* By being alert, you will accomplish more.

Rest. Of course, it is easier when your mind and body are running at optimal performance. If you are physically or mentally tired, rest! Do not rest for only a few minutes, thinking you will be rejuvenated. Begin taking time out of each day to do fewer tasks so you have time to reconnect with yourself.

Chapter 9: Phase 3- ⊛ - Organize

Finally, the topic you all have been waiting for: ORGANIZING! Many people associate organizing with getting rid of unneeded objects, but it is not. Organizing is creating structure and order.

Now that you have gotten your time under control, you can begin to organize your space and information. In the *Stabilize* phase, the Zone Defense of organizing was described and you should have identified zones that are congruent with your needs. Now that you have learned to prioritize and schedule the undone tasks so that they are no longer cluttering your mind, you can concentrate at looking more closely at each zone and get truly organized.

There are many books on getting organized so much of this may already be written somewhere else but as a professional organizer, people often ask me how I know what to do. As I thought about the process, I realized that I am consistent with my methodology. I hope sharing my consistent systematic activities will help you on your journey.

✂ Activity: Zone Detail Worksheet

A Macro Sort is one in which you separate something into broad categories. In the previous chapters, you have macro sorted tasks and their corresponding information. In this chapter, the "something" being sorted will be physical items.

As you sort, you may notice that like items are scattered throughout your physical environment and are not all gathered in one location. Often this is done by default without any conscious thought. If you have consciously created the multiple locations, the reasoning may be that there is not enough space in any one location. In other words, items end up in multiple locations and it is easier to leave them there than to merge them. So creating broad categories will allow you to evaluate like items as a whole. Upon evaluation and considering merging the multiple spaces, you may find that there are duplicates or that some of the items are not needed.

In this step, you only need to determine the larger categories. Later you will further subdivide the categories. For example, when starting the process of organizing the desk, all writing tools would be placed in one good-sized box without regard to what type (pen, pencil, or marker). Because all of the writing utensils from the entire living space are not yet gathered in one location, the micro sort of writing utensils would come after all areas have been macro sorted into broad categories.

When determining categories you may want to look at larger spaces as a whole. By seeing larger items that may unnecessarily be taking up space, for instance, you can quickly remove them to make space to work and sort. Using the basement, for example, you may see that unused furniture is a large category. By noticing this macro category, you may be able to arrange to have a charity pick them up before starting work on the basement corner by corner, space by space.

In the *Put Myself First* chapter, you created zones to help you become familiar with your individual needs. This is the time to determine what you want in each zone. Complete the **Zone Detail Worksheet** to list broad categories of items that you have and the zone where they belong. The exercise will take a while but will be worth the time spent. For reference, on average this process takes me about an hour. It will help you to take a critical look at your belongings so you can begin to see what types of things you tend to accumulate. This activity is NOT one in which you write down every single item you own. It is one in which you need only to look at the items in terms of the general categories.

To get you started, the common categories have been listed on the worksheet. For each category, simply choose a zone from those listed in the *Put Myself First* chapter and write the zone down next to that category. If some of your items will not fit into a category, list new categories at the bottom of the worksheet, and use additional paper if needed. However, I want to caution that you should not have too many groupings at this time.

Zone Organizing Detail Worksheet

Categories of Items Needed   **Zone:**

- ☐ Clothes/shoes
- ☐ Books
- ☐ Decorations
- ☐ Multi-media items
- ☐ Computer parts/equipment
- ☐ Sporting goods
- ☐ Games
- ☐ Magazines
- ☐ Mementos
- ☐ Household items
- ☐ Cool gadgets
- ☐ Collections
- ☐ Hobby items
- ☐ Children's toys/furniture
- ☐ Hair/beauty paraphernalia
- ☐ Furniture
- ☐ Lawn/garden/snow tools
- ☐ Building repair tools
- ☐ Paper items
- ☐ _____
- ☐ _____

Extras (list the categories of items that you have that don't belong in a zone)

_____

_____

_____

Novelty and play may help this process too. If you are more inclined, try using a hand-held voice recorder. Just name everything you see in the pile. It does not take long. One client said: "The strange combinations made me laugh and started a subconscious macro sort. I also heard my emotional reaction to some of the stuff, which was a great clue as to what was weighing me down."

My suggestion is to type the list so it can be sorted in different ways. Using this process also may create some healthy distance so you could review the category without emotional/visual associations. Also, categories that someone else such as a spouse may have to deal with could be reviewed in a concise manner and at their convenience without them getting into the dust and clutter.

Now that you have a general blueprint for all of the zones, you can use your prioritization skills as a guide to deciding what zone to tackle first. Set dates for each priority and transfer tasks to the appropriate task list. You now have a plan of action for your macro organizing. You may have to schedule your zones by how much space is available for sorting. You cannot spread out and sort if there is not an adjacent open space to use.

NOTE: Although the remaining activities are noted in sequential order, they may often be done simultaneously with each other and in conjunction with lightening the load. Sometimes, you may be evaluating, purging, and organizing all at the same time. However, when you are first starting, it may be easier if you complete one activity before starting the next. That way it will not be too overwhelming.

🖈 Tactic: Physically do the Macro Sort

This is it. Time to get your hands dirty! Many new to organizing start here but as a seasoned professional organizer, I know that having created a plan will provide a basis for the physical sorting.

1. **Select the Space.**

   Make the space you are working small enough to accomplish in three hours or less. For example, if you have decided to tackle the basement, you may want to first tackle the stairs. This will not only make room to remove larger items in the far recesses of the basement, it will be very motivating to see one space completed.

2. **Put Like Items Together.**

Look at the space and find like items and put them together. Simply take all items from one classification and put them in a box or designated space to keep them all together. Do not use them or stop to reminisce about when you received them. **Do not get distracted by making any determination about if you want to keep them or that they are broken.** The exception to this rule would be if you can throw them right into the garbage or donate box without much thought. The key here is to keep the momentum going and not stop to contemplate the merits of each item. Another way of looking at this step is that you are clearing the underbrush to see the trees.

To help you attain the skills necessary to categorize your belongings, it may be helpful to start big when putting like items together. For those of you who are not analytical, finding the common attribute may be tricky. Larger categories may be obvious like writing utensils and clothing. However, determining the more granular categories can be more challenging. Some examples of categories could be writing utensils, books, paper items, tools, makeup, and movies. If you are working on a child's space there may have categories such as cars, dolls, cards, building items, books, and papers.

This process of macro sorting could take a day, week, or even months. Keep using your Zone Detail list as a guide to making it through each zone. Don't get discouraged. This is the first step in funneling items to a manageable level.

Tactic: Create a Home or Zone

Although you may still have too many items, you should solidify which physical location for which the zone would be most effective. When deciding where to put each item, keep the following guidelines in mind. If you are having trouble visualizing how to fit the items into the space, call a professional organizer. It will be money well spent.

- **Store items for an activity in one central area.** For example, if you have some household tools in the kitchen and some in the living room and some in the garage, how will someone know where to return an item?

- **Group like items together.** For example, do not store toys in the children's rooms, some in the living room and some in the den. Store them all in one place and take them out when you need them.
- **Store items near where they will be used.** For example, if you do a lot of cooking and refer to cookbooks often then they should be stored near where you cook. If you rarely use a cookbook, they should be stored on the bookshelf in a "cookbook" zone or better yet keep two or three and donate the rest to the library.
- **Store things that will be used together in the same spot.** If they are together, you will more likely use them and avoid the frustration of hunting for a critical item. For example, store briquettes, lighter fluid, and matches with the barbeque grill.
- **Create a space for items in transition.** These are items such as library books, outgoing mail, etc.
- **Keep seasonal items in one area.** When summer items are outside, winter items would take their place in storage.
- **Assure accessibility.** For example, do not make your place for your pool toys in the attic where you will be spending an hour moving the Christmas decorations to find them.

⌂ *Never attempt this for another person without their consent.* Only organize your personal space and belongings. When determining the locations for items, remember you are only looking at general use household spaces. Each person should have their own space which is private and maintained by them alone.

🖥 Electronic Considerations: Creating Information Zones

When creating zones for information, be consistent with folder structure across all types of files. For example, if auto insurance paperwork is filed in a category with the label, "Insurance - Auto," then don't file the e-mail by name of the insurance agent.

Also, keep in mind that information consists of both paper and all electronic formats. Some examples of electronic formats are electronic documents, e-mail, and web favorites.

📍 Tactic: Put Items Away

Finally, time to physically organize. Not really. You may still have too much stuff to fit in the zones so you will most likely need to proceed to *Lighten Your Load* chapters.

This book will NOT show you how to make things look pretty. Refer to other organizing books and articles on how to utilize containers and make things aesthetically pleasing.

Taking it Deeper

In addition to having a spot for everything, systems should be set up to help you remain organized and ensure that every member of the household takes responsibility for maintaining order. By systematizing the trivial and routine tasks, you do not have to think about them and you will have time for more fun things. Systems will be addressed in more detail in the *Attain Equilibrium* chapter.

A note from the house manager:

Everyone needs to participate in the care and upkeep of our common environment.

Clean up after yourself. For example: when you brush your teeth, rinse out the sink!

If you take something out, put it away.

If you use a dish, wash it.

Notice your environment.

If you see something that needs fixing, fix it. Or tell the house manager about it.

In other words, care about the whole house, not just your personal space.

Chapter 10: 🕸 Lighten Your Load- Space

Although one can arrange a large number of items, it is more energy draining. The more you have the more you need. And the more you need, the more money you require. The more you own or are responsible for, the more time you need to clean it, repair it, and care for it. Being a caretaker of stuff can be a full-time job.

Many *Feng Shui* and organizing professionals will tell you that by eliminating clutter from your life you will be opening the way for new things and more energy. This means not just eliminating physical items but also ideas, emotions, and worn out relationships. It will give you lightness and confidence. You may have a hard time believing that this is possible, but it is true. Let me give you an example.

A woman got divorced and moved 500 miles from her home town. She did not get rid of anything. When she moved into her new place with a roommate, she agreed to pay for storing half of her things. Within six months they moved to a slightly larger place. However, she thought, "Bigger place! I can buy more." Her roommate would not let her clutter up the new house and forced her to make decisions about objects she already had. Three months after that, she moved to an apartment closer to work. Living on her own, she could not afford as much square footage and needed to cut back again on her belongings as well as get rid of her storage area.

Moving forced her to look at the items she had accumulated over the years. She had to decide, for example, if she should keep the monogrammed towels that had her ex-husband's initials or the framed wedding photos and invitations. Shedding personal belongings forced her also to look at the relationships she had in the past and those she was keeping currently. She realized her true friends were the ones that followed her address changes three times. Ultimately, her truest friend turned out to be the one person who helped her make decisions about what to keep and who helped move her belongings. The realization of what to keep and not to keep had liberated her and opened her up to let people (including herself) see the real her.

Are the items that you own considered clutter? The term clutter will be mentioned often in this chapter so it warrants a short discussion on what it is. Wikipedia, the on-line encyclopedia, defines it this way: "clutter is a confusing or disorderly state or collection, or the creation thereof." For example, clutter can be found in a drawer in which no defined set of items belong, or a pile in the kitchen on which there could be paper, batteries, a button, and an unopened granola bar. Although you may not think a space is cluttered, items within spaces often get blended. This would also be considered clutter.

Please keep in mind that you are not going to eliminate clutter and lighten your load overnight. You may not even accomplish this in one year. Use the tools you have learned about goal setting, scheduling, and setting priorities to set smaller tasks for yourself.

For example, I like to do needlework, mostly knitting and crocheting. So whenever I go to yard sales, I cannot resist yarn at a good price. Over the years I seem to have collected enough yarn that will keep me knitting continually for ten years and never have to buy more. How many sweaters does my family need? Using the goal setting and prioritization skills from this book, I made a pact with myself to make items for charity projects and resist buying any new yarn until all of the old yarn is used up. It will be hard and take time, but my basement will stop looking like a yarn store.

Being a professional organizer, I am much more organized and have less clutter than most. In life, I had been constantly purging the cursory stuff like clothes, books, and paper, but I always felt like it was a constant struggle to lighten my load. When I began whittling down my stuff as an almost empty nester, everything became so clear. I owned a large house to accommodate four children but as the CEO of the household, the common areas were all my responsibility. When the children started to move out I realized that those common areas had way too much stuff. So I started tackling the household stuff. I finally breathed a sigh of relief after I purged my sewing box which contained more thread than I could use in a lifetime.

If you are a young adult with a growing family, realize that you don't need all of the stuff that you think you need. The children don't care if you have an entire cabinet for arts and crafts. If they want to do arts and crafts they will find the supplies. One family that I was working with hired me to organize their belongings. Both parents were minimalists to the extreme that I may have trouble finding a writing utensil in the house. One day when I was working in the garage, I noticed cut up cardboard boxes all over the floor. Underneath them was a beautiful looking robot that the son had made. Unfortunately, he used the vacuum cleaner hose for an arm. Oops!

Also, the children don't care if you have three snowsuits for them. You do. Make sure your kids have something to keep them warm and bundle them up before they go out to make snow angels.

If you are a family with growing children, don't wait until the children are all grown to purge. Start getting rid of the stuff now. When a child outgrows one phase, don't hold on to the items (unless the next one is showing interest in the items). As my teenaged son told me, "I am no longer the eight year old who goes outside, rides his bike, and then comes in and plays with LEGOS (but you can't get rid of the LEGOS, smile)." Well, at least I can get rid of the now too small bike.

If you are approaching an empty nest or already there, now is the time to downsize. It is a process. Start with the big stuff. Get rid of furniture that is broken or that you don't like. If your children want something, give it to them now. Why wait until you die? They could be enjoying it now. Get rid of the items that you use for large family gatherings such as big soup pots. Donate or pass along office supplies, bags, good china, books, clothes, and toiletries.

As I continue to work with elders, I realize that they have called me to help purge because they have way too much and don't have the energy to do it themselves. I could go on and on about this topic, but the message is clear. No matter what stage of life, we could all stand to lighten our loads.

> "If you can't take care of it, you don't need it."

✂ Activity: Touch Every Item

Retrieve your listing of Macro Organizing Rules and keep it handy to remind you of the decisions you made earlier. Grab a writing utensil and keep it handy so you can add rules as you go along. Put down all other papers and lists so your hands are free to go through each space and physically touch every item.

Plan to tackle one zone at a time. If you have ten zones you should plan at least ten days (they do not have to be consecutive). Remember, during the planning, zones were broken into three-hour increments. Even if one zone takes one hour, do not try to tackle another one on that day. Reward yourself for a job well done.

As you touch each item, evaluate its value in your life.

☝ **Do NOT leave the zone, during the decision-making portion of the process.** It will waste time and ultimately distract you.

📌 Tactic: Evaluate Item

Now that you have a good idea of the categories of items and have taken an initial sweep at sorting them, you can begin to evaluate the items that you have and need. In this step, you are learning to evaluate and make decisions. Here are some guidelines to use when deciding what to keep.

1. **Item is used regularly**. What is regular? Certainly using an item daily, weekly, or monthly is regular. However, if you use an item only once a year, you may decide that yearly is regular, too. The determination will be made based on space and importance to you. For example, although you may only use a power washer once a year, it is a costly item that if rented once a year would cost more than purchasing it once.

2. **The amount of space it takes up is proportional to its value.** For example, you have a rowing machine and you use it once every three months when you decide to get in shape. In the narrow sense of the word, you are using it regularly.

However, it takes up space in the living room where you and your family sit daily to relax and unwind and you only have enough space for the family and cannot have guests over because there is no room for extra seating in the living room. If creating relationships is valuable to you, then the value of the rowing machine may be less than that of extra seating.

3. **The item has sentimental value.** Sometimes items are saved merely because they remind you or a family member of something special. However, sometimes you may say that something is sentimental, but you are delaying the uncomfortable emotions that would be evoked if you purged the item from your possession. It may be easier to keep the item than deal with the emotions that you have to experience upon letting it goes. Just do it! Prepare yourself and bite the bullet. Be careful not to attach sentiment simply because you own an item.

4. **Item is needed for a current or upcoming project.** For example, I am working on a crocheting project and have had my crochet bag next to my desk for about six months. The crocheting is a current project, but, obviously, I am not very interested in completing the project. When clearing my desk area, I would need to decide if the project is still important, and if yes, decide on a permanent location for partially completed crochet projects.

5. **More time is spent storing, fixing, cleaning, or maintaining the tool than the benefit it provides.** Examples of these types of items that are designed to simplify a process or make it easier to perform a task are blenders to weed-whackers. They are only beneficial to keep if they do not complicate your life.

6. **Item is a duplicate of a similar product.** The question could be phrased slightly differently. Could another item be used to achieve the same task? Although there may be a slightly different feature on a similar product, think about the use. For example, if you have a food processor and a blender that has a food processing attachment, the food processor can be considered a duplicate.

Some other common questions to ask when evaluating an item are listed below.

- Is it in working condition?
- Is it expired?
- Does it put my family's health in danger?
- Do I keep it out of guilt?
- Is it too specialized?
- Does it truly save time?
- Do I keep it because everyone has one?
- Could I use this space for something else?
- Is it still valid in my life?
- Would you want to carry it up three flights of stairs?
- Is the item worth the trouble?

As you move through your own organizing, beware of the thought, "I might need this someday." Much of the time you will not use it again. Ever. It may be cluttering up your space and preventing you from getting the things you really need.

When on the fence about whether you need something remember this adage, **the Universe provides**. What does this mean? If you are holding on to something because you might need it someday chances are you won't need it. And if you do, it will come your way again at that time. This is a small example, but very relevant. I was going grocery shopping and had a long list. I got to the store and realized that I forgot a pencil to cross items off the list. Lo and behold on the ground in the grocery store was a pencil. That was a small example, but what about you? You are saving some cables in case you move and need to hook up a second TV in the other room. Currently, you don't even own a second TV. Or are you saving a beautiful dress that your mother made, in case you have a child that will wear it? Chances are, the child will be a boy, it will be out of style, or you won't even have children and it was all for naught. Personally, I was saving many of the books that I used to read to my children when they were small. While in the process of downsizing, someone asked why I was saving all those books. And I said, "Maybe someday I will read them to my grandchildren." He replied, "of course, when you have grandchildren, you will get more books at that time." I could give thousands of examples, but you get the idea; you are holding on to these things in case "someday" happens.

To decide what to eliminate, you could just shut the door and walk away from it all. Of course, I am joking. You most likely cannot pack up and move on the spur of the moment or just throw everything away. But you can pretend that you are moving cross-country to an abode

that is half of the size as the one in which you are currently living. Keep in mind that in a real move, you would be paying for each pound of transported stuff. Ask yourself, "Would I want to spend money to carry that item with me? You will be amazed at how much stuff you can eliminate.

It boils down to one bottom-line question. **Does the item connect you to a feeling you want to perpetuate, regardless of time and space?**

A Note about Collections

Once you begin to sort items, you may realize that you have enough of one category to consider it a collection that you may want to display together. Or you may have intentionally or accidentally been acquiring a collection of particular types of items or relating to a topic or category. As you begin the process of evaluating your belongings take a hard look at your reasons for the collections. How did it start originally? How did it grow? Was it intentional because you loved the category? Or did someone give you the items and it kept growing? Do you need the essence of the item in your personal sphere now or have you outgrown it? For example, you may have started collecting owls because you are a teacher and a student gave you an owl figurine that you left on your desk. Then another student saw it and thought you liked them so they got you one. And before you know it you have 100 owl items. When you think about it, you don't even care for owls but you feel bad getting rid of them. It is okay to photograph the collection and let it go.

🕯 **Tactic: Place Item in Sorting Area**

Use the following suggestions to help you with decisions on which area an item should be placed.

- **Junk/Trash:** You clearly do not need it. It is old/expired or broken beyond repair. During the weeding out process, your best tool for this area will be a trash can. We all have them. Do not be afraid to use one. In this exercise, it is best to use a kitchen size trashcan that will be big enough to freely discard items, yet small enough to be able to lift out of the house. Keep the trashcan and strong drum-sized bags in this area.

- **Recycle:** Recyclable items should be included in the trash section and should be sorted according to the town's recycle collection policies.

- **Donate/Sell:** It is still in good condition and someone else could use it. Many items can be classified in this category. You will be amazed at the items that local charity organizations will take. Newspapers, old blankets or moth-eaten wool sweaters (animal shelters), appliances, tools (homeless shelters), books, and videos (local libraries), for example. Clothing can go to charity or can be sold at a consignment shop. If you invest the time, about 90% of your discards can find good homes. Keep trash bags and/or boxes in this area ready to fill. Some people find clear bags are useful to differentiate donate/sell from trash.

- **Repair:** "I want it and need it and love it, but it needs a minor repair." If something is going in this pile you need to *set a time limit* that it will stay in a state of disrepair. For example, if you do not fix your broken snowblower by the end of winter, you may not ever need it.

- **Move the items to a new location:** It would be better stored or used in some other location. For example, coasters were a good idea to store next to the cups and glasses but they may be better near the end table in the living room. Do not move it now, just keep these items in the area for moving to a new location.

- **Not sure**: Not sure if I need it; not sure if it belongs here. Try to decide in 30 seconds. Time yourself and at the end of 30 seconds, if you cannot find reasons to keep it, then toss it. If you cannot decide and feel uncomfortable about tossing it, put it in a "not sure" box to be looked at again. If the "not sure" box is large, it may be time to get objective outside help for decision-making.

- **Keep in this zone:** It makes sense to store this item here. It is located where it will be used. There is room for it in this zone. If it makes sense to keep the item in this zone but all items will not fit comfortably into the space, each item will need to be re-evaluated.

⚡ Tactic: Clean Up Sorting Area

After everything has been sorted, you have reached the long-awaited moment to take action in each area.

- **Junk/Trash:** Take the trash out of the area and put it in a staging area for final removal – trash area, curb, or car to carry to dump.
- **Recycle:** Take the recycling out of the area and put it in a staging area for final removal.
- **Donate/Sell:** Box or bag the items going to charity and move it to a staging area for final removal. Write a task on your task list to either call someone to remove it or bring it to the collection site. See the list at end of this chapter for ideas on where to donate items. Yard sale items would go in this area.
- **Repair:** Move the items to your "WIP" area. For each item write a task on the appropriate list that will remind you to repair the item and write "(WIP)" after the task so you remember where you put the item needing repair.
- **Move to a new zone:** Move the items to the new zone. If that zone has already been organized, then put it in the exact location within the zone. Otherwise, just place it in the zone and move on. You will deal with it when you are organizing that zone. Sometimes moving items to a zone that has already been organized will cause you to have to re-organize that entire zone. If this is the case, do not stop now to re-organize the zone. Add re-organizing that zone to your task list.
- **Not sure:** Box up these items and store in a designated area that you will organize toward the end of this process. Make sure you have a task on the list for this "decide later" zone.
- **Keep in this area:** Ok now is the time you can organize and make things look pretty. My guess is that you are tired from the above so schedule another time to organize this area.

✦ Tactic: Remove Items Not Staying

Don't be lazy and just put the items in the garage or basement and forget about them. If you don't remove the items then you will get right back in the same mess. Schedule time for it.

Notes about Donations

Often you may think that no one would want the items you are discarding. However, you can find charities for most if not all of the items you no longer need. For example, local animal shelters often need old newspapers, pet toys, blankets, sheets and even writing utensils. Senior centers are often good places for bringing magazines, books, and yarn. Schools often need small items that they can use for craft supplies. Shelters take many household and personal items such as lamps, blenders, and clothing.

Sometimes charity could be family members or friends. For example, a student just graduating and starting out with their first apartment may need dishes, household gadgets, and towels. Or family members may be interested in the hutch cabinet handed down from your great grandmother.

There are so many organizations asking for donations, it may seem impossible to decide where your stuff should end up. There are ways to ensure that your donation is going where you feel it will do the most good. So consider the following when choosing.

Decide The Criteria That Are Important To You. There are no wrong answers. Is it local, national, or international? Is it associated with various causes such as educational, medical, the arts, or a particular religion?

Decide The Number Of Charities That You Want To Support. Some people find it easier to use one or two, while others want to spread their donations over several organizations.

Important! Always research the charities. Charities may not take certain types of items. Check with them before you set out an item.

♀ Taking it Deeper

Obviously, you cannot discard everything, but you can work at fixing or replacing your belongings with items that you love and want to keep forever. If you were in business, you would not want too much inventory because you would be losing profits by having items sitting on your shelf. Nor would you want too little inventory that you would need to pay premium prices to manufacture the product when orders came in. The same is true of personal space. You do not want to tie up your money purchasing items that you feel you must have but only can use once in a while. Nor do you want so few possessions that you are required to pay premium prices to immediately buy something when you need it.

For example, one woman wanted to make sure she had enough baking mixes on hand just in the event her teenage daughter was in the mood to bake. However, when talking with her daughter about why she never baked, the daughter stated that she was never sure how old the eggs in the refrigerator were so she didn't want to take any chances. After her daughter went to college, the woman ended up throwing out thousands of dollars' worth of outdated food.

Think about how many square footage your real estate bill is paying for and how much is unusable due to the junk that is on it. How much would you pay per month if you had to rent storage space for the same amount of square footage lost to unnecessary items? An activity you can do to get your wheels turning is to tour a small house that is being shown to sell and try to visualize your stuff in it.

Typically, people do not edit their belongings until they are forced to. Since I cannot be there with you, try this next exercise I did with my high school church group and have used it with groups for years. **Assuming your family and friends are safe, if your house was on fire and you got to keep five (5) things what would they be?** This exercise for some people may create raw panic because they begin thinking of all the things they should take if there were an emergency. It is not intended to help you organize for disaster or solve some issues such as what to do about electronic back up for essential files. Instead, it is designed to help you figure out what is truly important in your life. Some answers that people initially list are iPod, computer, and cell phone. Hopefully, this helped you realize that these items and others like money and clothing can be replaced. If you had the benefit of group discussion you may realize that since you can only take five items, non-

replaceable items such as heirloom jewelry, scrapbook and photos may be better choices. Since becoming an organizer, I have put identification as the number one item on my list.

✂ Activity: Consider Why You Keep Stuff

Fill out the **Why Do You Keep Stuff Worksheet** to help you examine why you keep things. The checklist lists some common reasons people hold on to items.

Check all that apply:

- ☐ I may need it later (aka just in case).
- ☐ It holds sentimental value to me.
- ☐ I do not want to waste it.
- ☐ Someone gave it to me, and I don't want to hurt their feelings.
- ☐ It helps me remember something (trip, year, etc.).
- ☐ It makes me feel worthy and it gives me status.
- ☐ It is broken and needs to be fixed.
- ☐ I bought it. I need to get my money's worth.
- ☐ I inherited it. it must be important.
- ☐ It is my visual history.
- ☐ It can be useful to solve another problem.
- ☐ The activity that I use it for is important but there is no space.
- ☐ I love it so much I bought many of the same item.
- ☐ If I throw it away, I may throw away part of myself.
- ☐ It needs protection.
- ☐ I am nervous about letting go of it.
- ☐ I never really thought about it.

This questionnaire may bring the realization that you may hold onto things for illogical reasons. People often own things that they feel will create a sense of control over their lives. By holding on to all the stuff, they are hiding from their true selves.

You do not need things to give you a sense of control. Now is the time to look to the present, rather than keeping things to reassure you of who you were.

🔖 Tactic: <u>Identify If You Value Stuff vs. Experiences</u>

Are you a person who values the experiences that you have had? When you go on vacation do you purchase souvenirs to remember the experience? Are the traditions that you have with your family the most memorable part of the holidays? If you answered YES to the above, then you probably value experiences more than the stuff related to them. Then why do you have so much stuff? How can you possibly have time for experiences if you are too busy caring for your stuff? Purge it so you can stop spending time caring for it and start spending time enjoying experiences.

When you have the time, you can be fully present. You don't have to be distracted by the devices and paper drawing you in to the technocratic world. You can notice the scene, the fallen tree that you are passing, or the sadness of a person you are with. You can take in the scents of your surroundings such as the cinnamon spice on your coworker's snack or the dampness in the air. When you don't have to constantly be checking devices and completing tasks, you can relax.

① Quick Hits

Many of these can become rules that you add to your rule sheet.

- **Make choices.** In an earlier chapter, we learned about making choices with time. This is the same skill.
- **Live with your decisions and choices.** Do not agonize over whether you made the right choice. Do not constantly second-guess yourself and try to make a new choice.
- **Continually purge.** There are many suggestions on how often and how much to purge at a time.

⇧ **Put things away when done with them.** When you are done with something each day, put it back where it belongs. For example, if you take the few extra seconds to return your shoes to the closet, you will not waste time searching later, and your house or zones will be neater. I know this is hard if you live with an eternal slob. The best you can do is accept the fact that the place for unfinished magazines is on the floor next to the couch. Remember this rule: You can only organize yourself.

⇧ **Eliminate acquiring.** Buy only what you need. Think before you spend. When you are considering buying something, before bringing it into your possession, decide how often you anticipate using it and where it will be stored.

⇧ **Do not accept gifts that you do not need.** Or accept them but give them to charity or to someone who can use them.

⇧ **Say "NO" to telephone solicitors** trying to sell you something. The magic phrase is "Please take my name off your list" or else they will call again.

⇧ **Do NOT clutter a space**, especially after it has already been de-cluttered.

Chapter 11: ✦ Lighten Your Load- Information

Here is a silly thought I had one day when sorting through one person's lifetime's worth of various greeting cards they had received: if you track all the people who gave you cards during your lifetime, you might be able to analyze trends. For example, you may find out about demographics, groupings, and quantity. That could be important. Right?!

In this chapter, I challenge you to take a hard look at the paper and electronic e-mail and documents in your possession so you can lighten your information load. Do you need to hang on to those diaries you wrote when you were 16? Or can you just pull out a few select pages and set a date for scrapbooking them or creating a journal to show your kids what you were like when you were their age? When deciding on eliminating paper or electronic documents, you will not only need to consider its purpose in your life as you did with space, you will also need to address your comfort factor about the ease of finding it again from other sources. Additionally, consider that certain records will need to be stored on paper and quickly retrievable in case of an emergency.

At the beginning of the information age, people were just learning about what information could be made available. As time progressed, and as more and more information was stored on computers, they began hoarding the information on their electronic devices, just in case someone asked them a question and they forgot the answer. As information was pushed out to the internet and made available to all, it has no longer been important to keep information in the local environments because information can be retrieved at a moment's notice.

However, this influx of articulable information has increased the amount of paper being disseminated into workplaces and homes. Much of the paper funneling into the personal space is unsolicited but that does not mean it should be left unprocessed.

So where should you start? Make a commitment to lighten the load of information that your brain has to process. Stop watching multimedia, listening to music, reading books, and viewing magazines. In other words, shield yourself from the vast amount of information that is in this world. Many people would not make that kind of commitment and think that suggestions are un-realistic, so I propose that you start to minimize the amount of paper and digital information you receive.

🔖 Tactic: Minimize Unsolicited Paper

Mail needs the most prompt action. Do not pick up the mail, see what is good, and put it down to resolve later. As you receive a paper, decide right away if you are going to need it. An incoming mail pile can be pared down drastically with very little thought. I work with countless people on wading through mounds of paperwork that they have accumulated. The sad news for them is that about 80% of the mail I open is unsolicited. In other words, they are paying me to open their junk mail. If you can pledge to get through the backlog and keep mail current then you can take it to the next step of minimizing unwanted mail.

Spend time to remove your name from marketing lists. Writing to or calling any of the current "DO NOT CALL" lists is usually ineffective. The best way to get results is to contact the individuals who sent you the unsolicited mail. It may seem tedious, but in the end, it will be worth the effort.

Even after taking those actions, lightening the paper load battle remains. You will magically find other places to get paper such as places like rest areas, the library, and storefronts. Another big paper item that will grow if left unattended are magazines. Be cognizant of these types of papers that make their way into your possession and try to minimize them.

🖥 Electronic Considerations: Minimize Junk E-mail

Viewing e-mail on the phone or other handheld device is not conducive to marking e-mails as spam or clicking on the "unsubscribe" button of bulk e-mails. Also, when busy, who has the time to even think about it? So schedule time at your desk for these two important tasks. A session to mark e-mails as spam and/or unsubscribe to bulk e-mails could take as little as 15 minutes but can save countless hours of wading through the subsequent e-mails.

🔖 Tactic: Evaluate Each Paper

Just as you did with physical items, go through each paper and evaluate its usefulness in your life. At this stage, just decide on the fate of a piece of paper. Don't waste time creating files for the papers being retained. Many people would argue that this method is inefficient because you are handling a piece of paper more than once. However, it is more efficient because your brain is thinking of evaluating and not switching gears to make any other decision.

Review the **Paperwork Decision Flowchart (p. 93)** as a refresher on how to evaluate each piece of paper. If after referring to the Paperwork Decision Flowchart, you are having trouble making quick decisions about a paper, keep it. Remember the funnel analogy. This might be the first pass at eliminating paper. You can always streamline later.

During the evaluation process, you will encounter a category of paper supplies such as manila folders, hanging folders, spiral pads, 3 ring binders, envelopes, and blank paper. At this point, merely place all supplies together in one area and then during or after the filing stage, you can decide what to keep.

If you have an overabundance of backlog paperwork, don't panic. Remember the lessons in the previous chapters. Schedule time for working on backlog. When you get to the appointment on your calendar, quickly do a macro sort to eliminate the obvious junk based upon the rules you identified for your inbox called: "Personal Rules for Putting Items into the inbox." If a paper falls into one of the categories that you would no longer put into the inbox, then follow the protocol on the rule sheet – toss, shred or recycle. Don't hesitate to add rules to the list as needed.

🖥️ Electronic Considerations: Evaluate E-mail and other Electronic Documents

Keeping your inbox full is like taking all of the papers around your house and putting them on your desk or kitchen table. If you do not have a system of filing them, they are much harder to retrieve. Therefore, an electronic e-mail Inbox should NOT be used to store e-mails that have been read and already acted upon. It should only be used for receiving e-mails that require action. In other words, the e-mails should be evaluated using the same methodology as used for physical paper, thus leaving the inbox empty at the end of the evaluation process.

I would be remiss if I only addressed e-mail as a source of incoming electronic information. Files can come into your space from opening a link on the internet or receiving them via a disk or other storage device. No matter what source, consideration of its use should be given to the file before committing it to permanent electronic storage area.

If you are deluged or overwhelmed, start by saving/backing up everything, including your "Downloaded Items" folder to an external hard disk that you can go through little by little. Just remember to enter a task on your Future Task list as a reminder to integrate processing this backlog into your organizing sessions with yourself.

Please note that the difference with e-mail vs physical paper is that it is easier to file it at the same time that the decision is made on what to do with it. If that process will require too much brainpower or will be too time-consuming, create a folder in the inbox called "To Be Filed." Then, schedule a task or calendar appointment with yourself to file the e-mails. I also have a folder for staging e-mails that have attachments that I want to save. Then I schedule the time to actually detach the files and store them appropriately.

If you are starting with a large backlog of e-mails, follow the process below to purge the e-mails that you no longer need. In the electronic world, you won't do a macro sort in the same way as you did for physical items and paper because during the purge phase you will learn to sort in different ways to make purging faster. Please note that the below are only a few of the myriad of suggestions available for cleaning up the inbox. There are multiple ways to accomplish many tasks on the computer.

1. **Use Clean-Up Command if Available.**

    Microsoft Outlook, for example, has a command than can do the first purge for you. Depending upon the version, navigate the home tab in the delete group and click "clean up." Click "clean up conversation." All redundant messages will be deleted. Don't worry about losing attachments. Outlook will save both e-mails if one has an attachment but the more recent one does not. (Microsoft, 2020)

2. **Delete Bulk and Junk E-mail.**

    After that, or first, if you are not using an application that has clean up command, sort the inbox by "from" and bulk delete e-mail from "junk senders." To highlight a bunch of e-mails at the same time, check on the first one in the group, hold down the shift key on the keyboard, and at the same time click on the last one in the group thus highlighting a whole bunch at the same time. Now press delete key on the keyboard.

3. **Delete Old E-mails.**

Next sort by date and delete e-mails past a certain date. Six months is more than a reasonable amount of time. If you are afraid that you might need to reference older e-mails, then skip this step and wait until you move important e-mails to file folders before deleting old e-mails.

4. **Clean Up Pre-Existing E-mail Folders.**

If you already have created folders in your e-mail system, use this time to evaluate them, and purge e-mails and folders no longer needed. For example, you may have created a folder for all e-mails related to a trip you were taking, but two years later, the folder and all e-mails are still intact.

5. **Evaluate Individual E-mails.**

Hopefully by this time you have weeded out enough e-mails that you are not overwhelmed with the volume and can start individually evaluating them.

✦ Tactic: Determine Zone Detail for Papers

Now that you have gone through the pile and hopefully decreased it to a manageable level, it is time to identify the file folders needed for papers being retained. Up until this point, the only papers addressed have been those that have a task associated with them. The papers to be tackled now are those that are being retained for reference.

It is best to categorize files by role. For example, home in one section, work in another, and personal interests in another. See the following for some common categories. For ease of visualizing the way this will work, consider that each category will be housed in one drawer of a file cabinet. For example, if you have four categories you will need four drawers in one or more file cabinets.

- **Tasks**

  Papers that you will need for accomplishing tasks within the next day, month, or year. This could be stored in the A-Z, 1-31, or other task files created previously. It could also include folders for task categories such as Errands, Phone Calls, Unpaid Bills, To Read, and Forms to Fill Out.

  I often recommend that a separate set of folders be created for current year paid bills and other financial paperwork that will be used for tax preparation purposes. Some of the specific files within this category could be bank statements, credit card statements, and medical explanation of benefits.

- **Home**

  Papers related to managing your home that may be needed for reference. Below are some common home categories. Please note that this is just a guideline because each person has a unique situation. When creating hanging folders consider the quantity of paper being filed into it. If there will be a lot for one, then don't hesitate to create a hanging folder for it. For example, some people may have many investments including a 401K or other retirement accounts. In this case, it may be better to create a separate category for investments. In this case, the hanging file would be labeled "Investment-Name of Investment Company."

Category	Paperwork Type
Auto	Vehicle Records
Banking	Bank Account Information
Financial	Credit Card/Loan Information
Financial	Credit Reports
Financial	Investments
Financial	Social Security Information
Health	Medical History
Home	Purchase/Sale/Deed/Appraisals
Home	Home Improvement
Home	Mortgage
Insurance	Home
Insurance	Life
Insurance	Medical

Category	Paperwork Type
Insurance	Vehicle
Legal	Accident Reports and Claims
Legal	Contracts
Legal	Lawsuits/Legal Correspondence
Legal	Will and Corresponding Documents
Personal	Activities
Personal	Certifications/Progress Reports
Personal	Important Documents*
Warranties/Manuals	Appliances
Warranties/Manuals	Child Products
Warranties/Manuals	Furniture
Warranties/Manuals	Tools
Warranties/Manuals	Misc. Warranties

*NOTE:

Important documents could include items such as a copy of driver's license, birth certificate, and marriage certificate.

- **Personal Interests**

  Papers that are of interest to you only such as gardening notes and knitting patterns. Some other common examples are Diet, Exercise, Education, Vacation, Music, Home Design Ideas, Fashion Ideas, Church/Religion, and Photos. This could also be a place to store special mementos.

- **Business**

  Papers that are related to your job or small business, if applicable. These are so varied that they do require specialization but for very small businesses I recommend the same categories as those used as business expenses for taxes. Examples could be Marketing, Utilities, Supplies, Employees/Subcontractors, and Licenses.

- **Archives**

  Papers that are related to assets that you no longer own but may need for reference or for financial information that may be needed such as tax records.

If you already have a reference filing system, this may be a good time to re-evaluate what files you are keeping and what files you need. Ask yourself these questions:

- Are there separate sections for home, business, and personal papers?
- When was the last time the folders were purged?
- Are there folders that were never used?
- Are the archives holding papers no longer needed?

As you are filing papers into the appropriate folders, you may realize that you need to further subdivide the category. For example, when working with older clients I have noticed that they need more health folders than younger people. It is common to create entire hanging folders for each body part. In this case, the hanging folder label would read "Health – Body part." As an example, write it like this: "Health – Eyes."

The suggested file folder worksheets can only give baseline suggestions. It will be up to you to figure out the "micro" details.

🖥 Electronic Considerations: Determine Zones for Electronic Documents

Use the same naming convention for filing electronic documents as those decided upon for paper.

🖥 Electronic Considerations: Determine Zones for E-mail

Always create a home or zone for what you plan on keeping. Create folders within the e-mail box with two zones for filing e-mails:

1. E-mails that need action
2. E-mails that no longer require action

Needs Action

E-mails needing action should be moved to one or more subfolders of the inbox, thus mirroring the physical Task Box or Drawer. More than one folder would be created when there are many e-mails related to one project or task. For example, if you are going on vacation and you have e-mails related to the various components of the trip (i.e. hotel, travel, entertainment scheduled), it may be easier to put them all in one folder until the trip is over. If a folder for a project has been created, do not forget to add a task onto the task list one of which should state "purge items from electronic project folder."

Alternatively, if you are using an electronic task list connected to an e-mail system, incomplete e-mails can be dragged to the task list.

No Longer Needs Action

E-mails that no longer need action but need to be retained for reference purposes should be stored in subfolders not within the Inbox section of the e-mail platform. Some common sections in which to create folders are Archive, Completed, and Folders. For these e-mails, create a subfolder by subject or topic. It will make for easy retrieval if the e-mail folder names are as similar to the paper ones as possible.

✒ Tactic: File Paper

I recommend folders, rather than binders, because they are more easily retrievable and hold more paper in a small amount of space. When creating labels, don't get fancy. You will most likely have changes. Handwrite the labels in pencil. I often use sticky notes as labels on each folder until I have finalized it. When inserting a plastic label holder into the slot of the hanging folder, it is recommended that they align in a row- not staggered. This allows for ease of finding the folder because the eye only needs to travel one row when searching. Whether you put the tab in the front or the back of the hanging folder is a matter of preference. If in front you will be in the habit of looking behind it. If in back, you may be able to put your hand on the label as a place holder while you look for info.

Finally, consider where on the folder the label should be placed. Should the hanging folder tab be on the right or left or somewhere in the center? I would recommend center if you are using a tall file cabinet and there is a long row of them. Otherwise, I recommend flush left or flush right depending upon how the drawer is situated in relation to where you will be when you are retrieving files. You want the label closest to where you will be sitting or standing. For example, if it will be in the desk drawer to the left of the chair, place the labels on the right-hand side of the folder.

Whether to use a cabinet, plastic tote, or pretty boxes is a matter of preference and space. Just make sure that the hanging folders can sit comfortably inside the container. If the file cabinet does not have the wire rack, get one. Don't try to make files stand up without one. Think twice before buying a pretty box if it is not designed for hanging folders. You will find yourself discarding it because it is not functional. As far as lateral or vertical file cabinets, vertical are a little easier to maneuver and they usually can be tucked away in tighter spaces.

When filing, think about the size of the paper. Although nowadays there is not much printed on legal paper, if you do get legal sized papers, consider folding it. If you have many small pieces of paper such as greeting cards or business cards; file them in a hanging folder with pockets and/or sides. After everything is filed you can now make pretty typed labels with your computer or label maker.

🖥 Electronic Considerations: File E-mail

Drag the saved e-mails into the appropriate folders as needed. Utilize skills learned previously to make meaningful categories. As you are dragging e-mails to folders, decide if these e-mails are truly needed and delete any that are no longer relevant.

🖋 Tactic: Remove items not staying in your possession

Don't forget to recycle and/or shred paper that you are not keeping. You can usually find inexpensive shredding options through senior centers, your local financial professionals, or town. Many office supply stores and printers also offer shredding options for a fee. If you want to shred paper yourself, invest in a micro-cut, cross-cut shredders to prevent would-be thieves from stealing your information. If you are conscious about the environment, many humane societies will take shredded paper for animal bedding.

🖥 Electronic Considerations: Remove E-mails Not Being Kept

Delete e-mails as you no longer need them but make sure to periodically delete the trash e-mail box as well as the sent e-mail box. Please note, when a project is completed, its folder should be purged before moving any permanently retained e-mails to its corresponding completed folder. The ultimate goal is to purge regularly so the e-mail inbox does not get overwhelmed.

To save partial information from an e-mail, forward e-mail to yourself and remove all of the information that is not needed. Another option is to copy and paste the information to a text document that would be saved with other electronic files.

Lighten Your Load With Laughter!

💡 Taking it Deeper

Part of lightening the information load will be to detox from mindless, disjointed activities. Life is so segmented, it is hard to be in the moment when you are constantly in a transitory state waiting for the time of the next scheduled activity. So many people fill their fragmented time playing video games, scrolling through their phones on social media, or reading endless novels.

The detoxification might look like this. I walk by the electronic device and check to see if I received any messages. Great, no message, now I have time to do something else. However, I have to go somewhere in two hours so I can't get too involved in a project. So I do house chores; dishes, laundry, pick up clutter, etc. Okay, that took twenty minutes, now what? Let me check my e-mail just to see if someone needs me. Answer a few e-mails. Okay, that took five minutes. Let me prepare food for later so I won't have to rush then. Move laundry to dryer. Now I have time to finally look at the crossword puzzle from the Sunday newspaper. Check e-mail again. Nothing. Maybe someone sent me a message on social media. Let me check that just in case. . . .

Lightening the information load may also entail letting go of the busyness of performing endless tasks that benefit what is perceived as "progress." Unfortunately, progress within the technological world is taking us away from living our true nature as human beings. Before computers and the internet, how did people get information? From the universe around them. As more information is shared, humans are losing the ability to get information from their senses. Instead, they try to follow the wisdom that others are preaching.

Stop listening to all those other people and listen to yourself. For example, instead of watching the TV to learn about the weather, go outside. Practice turning off your device. Put away books. Turn off the television. Turn off the radio. Clear your calendar and allow yourself to take the day as it comes. Listen to the cues your body tells you. Embrace the people that you come across and enjoy their gifts. Get in nature and learn what it has to offer.

Spend time being creative. If your mind is too tired to think about new ideas or learn new concepts then you may have information overload. It may be that you have polluted your mind with so much junk that it cannot think clearly. An easy place to start might be to weed out the everyday things that add clutter to your mind such as watching endless television shows, driving with the radio blasting loud music, or spending every free minute talking to others on the phone. Instead of doing those activities, take time to rest your mind or just plain think.

✂ Activity: Unweave Your Web of Responsibility

Think of your responsibilities like a web that has been woven since birth. You started with the responsibility to your family. Then as you went through adolescence you had other responsibilities and at some point, you wanted to break away and most likely moved out on your own. With each change, you added to the web of your life. In order to lighten your load of

responsibility, you will need to un-weave that web.

Use the blank spider web to help visualize the components within your web. Draw or write words for each area of responsibility that you have in your life. Be specific in listing the component within the following categories: home, love, family, work, activities, and spaces or items such as home and vehicle. Don't forget to also consider responsibility for things such as family heirlooms and places such as small piece of land in Florida that your mother owned. Now draw lines to connect responsibilities that are related to each other. For example, family heirlooms may intersect with family as well as your home.

Just the exercise of listing people, places, and things and seeing where they intersect will start you on the path of unweaving the web of responsibility. It will be up to you to release them from your responsibility. The longer you have taken to weave your web, the longer it can be to untangle.

The following example will help you see the thought process necessary to let go of the responsibility. I had a client who I worked with on and off for five years- from aged 85 to age 90. Shortly after her 90th birthday, she asked me to help her with her schedule because she was not able to fit everything in. Among other things, such as slowing down with advanced age, we discussed letting go of unnecessary belongings so she could relax a little. Some of those unnecessary sets of items were several sets of china dishware that none of her four children wanted. Nor could she get any of her many grandchildren to commit to taking the responsibility to keep and care for them. She loved to throw dinner parties at which beautiful place settings were as important as the delicious food, but her sad realization was that none of the family members had the same passion. By holding on to the china, she was holding on to the responsibility of caring for each piece and that was one of the unnecessary responsibilities that were draining her precious energy.

My advice to her was to be okay with releasing these items to someone else who will love them as much as she did. Let go of controlling their fate and give them permission to have a good life somewhere else. Once she could do that then she could have one less responsibility and one less thing using her precious energy. After coming to that realization, at 91 she was able to spend her energy in much more important ways. She held a "cooking class" for her grandchildren so they could learn how to make her recipes that they all loved.

① Quick Hits

- **Keep only ONE master system.**
  - If you use a paper system of organization, do not use any follow-up system in an e-mail unless you reference it in your paper system.

    <u>Electronic</u>
    - **Listen to voice mail and decide immediately** what action you are going to take. Then make a note and file for a follow-up.
    - **Make e-mail folders for later follow up** by category or move to tasks by date. If you keep it in your inbox you will keep looking at the same thing over and over.

    <u>Paper</u>
    - **Handle paper once for evaluation.** When holding a piece of paper, decide on what needs to be done with it right away instead of looking at it and putting it down for later decision.
    - **Use the rip and tear method of reading when looking at magazines and periodicals.** If you see something that you want to read in-depth, rip it out and put it in a "Read" folder for when you have more time to concentrate. This way you are not carrying around all of the advertisements and unnecessary articles and you do not waste time flipping through to find the article again.

Chapter 12:  Attain Equilibrium

Congratulations! You are almost there. You have almost all of the tools to remain organized. You have learned to plan your day and week. You have taken a hard look at your belongings and hopefully eliminated the unnecessary. You are now ready for the final stage of micro organizing. It is similar to when I passed my first level in Tai Chi. I was all happy and my teacher said "Ok now you are ready to learn Tai Chi." This is only the beginning.

Keep in mind that when trying to bring an unconscious habit into conscious control, some system is better than no system and it may take time. There may be a learning period where it runs your life. Don't get discouraged. Eventually, you will find it can work and be maintained without a lot of thinking, tracking, planning, and extra time consumption. However, don't go so overboard that you lose the intended purpose. ***You should not use the systems if they are going to overtake you and run your life.*** If you are so preoccupied with using the food chart, for example, that you cannot enjoy eating, then do not use the tool.

The only way to stay on track is to consistently monitor progress and make adjustments where needed. Once followed consistently, using a system can help achieve balance. Therefore, the focus of this last step of S.I.M.P.L.E. Life Organization is equilibrium. In order to achieve equilibrium, you must look at your life as a whole. Your life is not a collection of unconnected parts; it is a whole.

In the past, time management literature has taught us how to achieve balance by compartmentalizing and carefully monitoring the hours put into each area of your life. Wellness is a term that was coined in the 1980s for a very old concept of being. It professes that one must balance six aspects of his or her life to achieve a high level of wellness. These six components are social, occupational, spiritual, physical, intellectual, and educational.

However, categorizing, whether by time units or aspects of life, is not natural and balance is different for everyone. It should be the responsibility of each individual to decide the level of each component that is necessary for their life. From herein, it is up to you alone to consciously decide where to spend your energy each minute of each day. When you begin with intentional living, it is easy to stay out of drama created by others and ignore what others are trying to force you to do because you are calling the shots.

You have hopefully begun to realize the importance of planning. When I took my first time management trainer certification course, it was drilled into my head that I should instruct my students to: **plan every year once a year, every month once a month, every week once a week and every day once a day**. Since then I have added: **plan every routine once**.

Once routines are on automatic pilot, future time and energy can be spent on the things that matter most. Routines should not only be made individually but also for shared environments. In a household or work environment, once a process is set, it shouldn't rely on a particular person. Anyone should be able to jump in and follow it. For example, when my daughter was in the hospital having heart surgery, my parents could jump right in and follow the routines in the household. My father commented on how easy it was because everything had its place and the other three children could guide him.

Let's start by examining the routines that you perform regularly.

✂Activity: Identify Regular Routines

Use the **Repetitive Tasks – Create a Routine Worksheet** to list the repetitive tasks that you perform regularly whether on a daily, weekly, or another basis. When filling out the chart, make certain to list the number of hours *per week* that each task takes to complete. For example, doing the dishes, in general, could take fifteen minutes per meal but may take longer if there were a larger number of dirty dishes created during meal preparation. In this example, use fifteen minutes as the average amount of time it takes to complete the task times three meals per day times seven days per week. This total would be 315 minutes divided by 60 minutes per hour or 5 1/4 hours. Some other examples of repetitive tasks are pay bills, shopping, lawn work, home maintenance, preparing clothing/laundry, and housecleaning. The repetitive life tasks worksheet is not a plan. It is simply a tool to help you identify the repetitive tasks in your life.

My repetitive life tasks	Daily (D) Weekly (W) Monthly (M) Quarterly (Q)	Time to complete *per week* (in hours)
Eating	Daily	
Preparing for bed	Daily	
Paying bills	Monthly	
House cleaning	Bi-Weekly	
Home administration	Bi-Weekly	
Preparing schedule	Daily	

Now that you have identified some of your repetitive tasks you can start making them into routines.

To set up a routine system you will *start with the end in mind*. If you need a system to make sure that your bills are paid on time, you need to start with a way to remind yourself a week before the bill is due. After setting the time aside to regularly perform the routine, you will need to figure out how the tasks can most efficiently be linked together to create a smooth, effortless sequence. For example, if you leave your house for work at the same time every day and there are several tasks you must perform before you leave the house, you can make them into a routine. See **Simple Daily Routine for Children** for a sample of a child's daily checklist. This routine worksheet helps the parent to perform his or her own routines and not have to remember what the child is supposed to be doing. It also gives autonomy to the child.

Simple Daily Routine for Children

	SUN	MON	TUE	WED	THU	FRI	SAT
MORNING							
Get dressed							
Make bed							
Put dirty laundry in hamper							
Eat breakfast							
Brush teeth							
Comb hair							
Wash face							
Put on socks and shoes							
Pack lunch							
Pack backpack							
AFTERNOON							
Unpack backpack							
Unpack lunchbox							
Have snack							
Do homework							
Practice instrument							
Clean room							
Do daily chore							
Exercise							
BEDTIME							
Put on pajamas							
Brush teeth							
Wash face and bathe							
Clean room							

The remainder of this chapter will be dedicated to showing you how to set various routines and stick with them by setting rules and being disciplined.

✎ Tactic: Prepare for the next day routine

One of the most important daily routines for life organization is to prepare for the next day. This is not optional and will take about 15 minutes. You may despair as you look around at the mountain of paper and clutter of unfinished jobs. However, trust that after you get caught up on backlog, this process truly does only take 15 minutes per day.

Do this at the same time each day. If you do not have time at the end of a day to perform this routine, do it first thing the next morning.

Follow the steps below to complete the S.I.M.P.L.E. cycle and be prepared for the next day.

1. **List Details For All Scheduled Time Blocks For The Next Day.** For the most part, this will be done as the appointments are made but it is good to review to assure any are not missed.

2. **Carry Forward Any Uncompleted Tasks From The Current Days' Task List.** Remember to use the notations (✓, x, or →) to signify what was done with the task. **Review Using the Task List if necessary.** Although there is no hard rule as to the number of days that something can be carried over, each time you see an item on the task list, re-evaluate the task to determine if it needs to be completed...ever. Guidelines for removing items from task list:

   - **Priorities Changed.** As I was editing this book, I realized there was no example listed for this so I went to my task book for an example. As you may remember from the beginning of the book, I am editing this during the 2020 COVID 19 pandemic. I had on my list to check out a kite festival in the next town over which would allow me to meet people in the area as well as enjoy an outdoor event. Now that my priority for events has changed to ones where social distancing is key, the kite festival is no longer a priority.

   - **No Longer Relevant.** For example, one person had on her list to go to the internet and research instructions on how to work a particular feature on a product that she owned. After a year of moving the task to new lists, she finally realized that the feature she had hoped to learn was not necessary for her use of the product.

- **Not Important Now.** One example of something that frequently gets put on and taken off my list without ever getting completed is finding a lower mortgage rate. I add the task to my list because someone says, rates are low. I make one call and find out mine is lower. However, I keep the task on the list because I want to check around and see if I can find a lower rate. Eventually, I take it off the list because I am tired of looking at it. Six months go by and the process starts all over again.

3. **Add New Items To The Inbox From All Sources.** Clear your desk by putting all papers in your inbox. Some sources that may have papers to add to your inbox may include but are not limited to: pants or coat pockets, handbag, lunchbox, cup holder in the car, and table at the entryway to home or office.

4. **Clear The Inbox.** Do this by following the process suggested in the *Slow Down* chapter. Remember, if you put a paper into your Task drawer it should have a corresponding task on the Task list. Now your desk and inbox should be totally clear of paper. If you are using an electronic task list, there should be no past due entries or any entries without dates.

5. **Look At Tasks For The Next Day And Decide Which Ones Can Realistically Be Accomplished Within The Day.** If there are tasks that you will not be able to accomplish on that day, change the date to one that you think you may be able to accomplish the task. Since people inevitably underestimate the time necessary to complete all of their tasks, I created the activity **Estimate Time for Tasks** as practice on estimating how long tasks will take. After going through that exercise, do not be deterred from adding the item to the list for a particular day because the task may take longer than the available time for a day. Making small steps each day toward completing a task is just as important as crossing completed tasks off the list.

6. **Prioritize and Sequence the Task List for the next day.** Do this by using the tactics learned in the *Prioritize* chapter.

✄ Activity: <u>Estimate Time for Tasks</u>

In general, estimating time for tasks should be done as part of planning for the week which should be done before the beginning of the week. Select a consistent time each week to schedule the tasks to be accomplished in the following week. Typically weeks span from Monday to Sunday; therefore, Friday evening, Saturday morning, and Sunday evening are times that would work well. Monday morning is NOT a good time to plan the week because by that time it has already begun and is already prone to interruptions.

To practice estimating time for tasks, follow the steps below.

1. Next to each item on your Task List, write down the estimated number of minutes it will take to complete the task. Be realistic.

2. Double whatever you wrote. In general, tasks take longer than people estimate for a variety of reasons such as interruptions and getting distracted.

3. Add all of the minutes for all of the tasks on the list.

4. Determine how much time you have to complete those tasks. Start with twenty-four hours in a day less eight hours for sleeping and three for personal grooming and eating. Then subtract other blocks of committed time such as work or school and commuting. For reference purposes, if you did not have any other blocks of time committed then you would have 13 hours which equates to 780 minutes available for completing tasks.

5. Subtract the total number of hours estimated for tasks from step three from those available from step four. If there is a negative number then readjust the task list by moving items to a future week or delegating the tasks so someone else if possible.

Be realistic. Do not plan too much or schedule too tightly that you do not have the flexibility to adjust your schedule for interruptions and unexpected events. If you consistently do not complete your list, you may be setting your expectations too high or trying to cram too much into one day. Repeat the **Estimate Time for Tasks** exercise as many times as needed until you begin to instinctively estimate time for tasks more realistically.

Your active workspace should be kept up daily. There will be days, however, when you will not have time to follow the **Prepare for the next day routine**. At minimum, you should clear your desk every day and set your priorities. For every missed day of the inbox clearing step, schedule an additional 15 minutes to the day it is being done. For example, if you have missed five weekdays and will be catching up on this step on Saturday, you should plan one and a half hours (15 minutes times six days). A brief daily task, when allowed to mount up, turns into a weekend project of significant size.

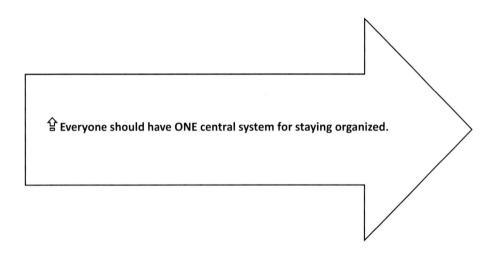

⇧ **Everyone should have ONE central system for staying organized.**

💻 **Electronic Considerations: <u>Routine for Using an Electronic Organizing System</u>**

Below are some modifications to the routine for use with an electronic organizing system.

1. **Verify all scheduled time blocks for the next day.** Confirm that all have been entered into the electronic calendar.

2. **Update the date on any uncompleted tasks.** This includes items from the current days' task list as well as any that were recently added that do not have any date listed.

3. **Add new items to the paper inbox.** Follow the same thought process as if an electronic organizing system was not being used.

4. **Clear both the paper and electronic inbox**.

    Clear the paper inbox before tackling the electronic inbox. To add items from e-mail to the integrated task list, simply drag e-mail from the inbox to the electronic task list.

    Once an e-mail is determined as needing action and the task is noted on the list, some consideration should be given to how to handle the original e-mail.

    - Decide if it will need to be referenced for the task. If yes, then it should be moved to the Task/Project subfolder within the inbox.

    - Decide if it will be needed for reference later. If yes, then it should be moved to the appropriate folder within the e-mail system.

    - If an e-mail will not be needed, before deleting, decide if any attachments will be needed. If yes, file them appropriately.

5. **Look at tasks for the next day and decide which ones can realistically be accomplished within the day.** Follow the same thought process as if an electronic organizing system was not being used.

6. **Prioritize and sequence the task list**. Many electronic organizing systems do not have the ability to number or sequence tasks. To get around this limitation, simply assign the numbers and letters at the beginning of the task description.

If you have more than one e-mail address or source of electronic tasks, decide which one will be the Hub of your organizing. After making that decision, forward any e-mails requiring action or filing to the e-mail account associated with the Hub. In other words, if you have work e-mail and home e-mail addresses and you have an item from work that needs to be acted upon at home, forward the e-mail to your home e-mail address so you can add the task to your task list.

✔ Tactic: Routine for Weekly Food Planning

Although you may enjoy taking short, frequent trips to the market, it is more time-efficient to go through the following process once per week. Add up the length of time it takes to drive to the store, push the cart through the aisles, stand in line (even if express), drive home, unload, unpack and put items away. Then multiply that by the average number of times per week you go to the market. If the sum of all days is less than one hour then don't change a thing.

Also, you may think that you will keep down storage overload and spoilage if you go food shopping more often. However, you can plan your menu around items that may need to be used up. When you begin using up items regularly, there is typically more room in the refrigerator for the frequently used items. Also, there may not be as many half-used jars and containers in the refrigerator. Planning also allows for more creativity in food choices. For example, I often go to the store and purchase a food choice that I think should be part of my diet such as canned oysters. Then I get home and realize that canned oysters are not one of my favorite foods. If I do not plan a meal around those oysters, they could be gathering dust on my shelf and using up space that can be better utilized for something I do enjoy and use more frequently.

One family I worked with had a stay-at-home dad who was happy eating a bowl of cereal with milk for every meal. Thus the mom always had to come home from a long day at work and cook a meal for her family. Upon discussion about their habits, we uncovered that the dad would gladly execute the plans if the mom and kids wrote down their menu selections. Once they put the routine in place, the family could enjoy a myriad of recipes.

If you need a little more convincing that routines are helpful for something as basic as eating and menu planning, then give the following routine a try. Decide on a specific day and time each week that this process will occur. Write this routine on your calendar so it will be on auto-pilot.

1. **Take inventory of what is on hand.** At some point, it would be helpful if you create a listing of what should be in your cabinets and refrigerator but don't feel that you need to create it before starting this process.

2. **Decide which items need to be used up within the week.** What has been in the cabinet or refrigerator for a while? Only select three items that fit into this category. If you select more you will not leave room for seasonal or on sale items. Nor will there be room for spontaneity or creativity. If there are more than three items that need to be used up, choose the ones that will spoil. Then you can save the others for future weeks.

3. **Create eight days of menus.** The **Simple Menu Planning Worksheet** was designed as a place to capture plans for daily food choices. Although there are seven days in a week, you should always make at least one extra day's worth of menus to leave room for choice and mood. Remember to revolve some of the menus around the three items that you chose to use up. For example, make breakfast for dinner one night to use up eggs.

Simple Menu Planning

Day of Week:
(circle one)

Mon **Tue** **Wed** **Thu** **Fri** **Sat** **Sun**

Item Category	**Item**	**Need to buy for this meal**
	Breakfast	
Grains		
Fruit		
Protein		
Beverage		
	Snack	
Fruit		
Protein		
	Lunch	
Grains		
Vegetable		
Protein		
Beverage		
	Dinner	
Grains		
Vegetable		
Protein		
Beverage		
	Snack	
Grains		
Beverage		

4. **Determine what needs to be purchased** to complete the meals planned.

5. **Determine if there are any staples** such as milk, eggs, and bread that are needed. Don't forget to look for non-perishable supplies like laundry detergent or light bulbs.

6. **Create a shopping list.**

7. **Shop** for the items on your list. While shopping, If you see something that looks appealing or is on sale, consult your menu list to see if it can be used that week or if it can replace an item already on the list.

8. **Put away groceries** in the appropriate location. If you have duplicates, practice FIFO (first in first out) method by putting the fresher item behind the previously purchased item. Write the date purchased somewhere on the item to catch the oldest of duplicate items.

✂ Activity: Planning Your Routines

Now that you have experienced the thought process for scheduling something as simple as meal planning, take time to create routines for each of the entries on the earlier created list: **Repetitive Task – Create a Routine**. Once identified, enter each one into the calendar.

See below for considerations about the frequency of routines.

- Daily. It would be best to perform it at the same time every day.
- Weekly. It would be best to do it at the same time every week. For example, block off one hour each Saturday morning for bill paying.
- Monthly. It would be best to plan the same day (second Monday) or date every month.
- Yearly. Use the future calendar as a place holder or set some sort of trigger to remind you to schedule an appointment. Some examples of triggers may be birthday, the first day of spring, or a particular holiday.
- Seasonal/Quarterly. Some examples are closing up the yard for the winter or paying yearly taxes. Optionally, you can make checklists by season. For example, a spring yard work checklist may include the following: get hose out, turn on the outside water, pick up sticks, rake yard and cut back bushes.
- Less regular routines. Use the **Less Regular Routine Chart** to list your less regular routines. Make sure to include personal routines that need to happen on a regular but not necessarily as routine a basis such as: getting a haircut, yearly physical, purchasing clothes, car service/oil change, holiday shopping, septic clean, oil burn clean, or piano tune.

Less regular routine:	Month to be Done:

When you are ready, use this list as a starting point for your routine manual.

Consider the weather and seasons when scheduling. For example, use summer as garage cleaning since working with the garage door open is like being outside and winter is a good time to clean out the storage area next to the boiler.

Another example of a yearly task that needs a reminder is cleaning out children's toy boxes and cabinets. A good time for this is before their birthdays. That way they can get rid of toys that they have outgrown. It is also a great time for them to rediscover toys that they may have forgotten that they had; so, when they are asking for new toys, they will realize that they do not need much. They may even realize that some purchases from previous years were wasteful, so they learn not to waste. Also, this is a way of knowing how much space they have for storing new things they receive for their birthday or holidays.

Be sure to include a routine for modification to each zone. At minimum, all zones should be weeded out once a year. For example, you could purge clothing during the change of each season or cull through books at the beginning of summer. Many people do this as a "spring" or "fall" clutter cleaning; however, if you have a large house and busy life, you cannot get it all done at once so it is best to schedule each zone as you did in the *Lighten Your Load* chapter.

Also, at least once every three months it is a good practice to periodically check your entire task list and reprioritize the tasks on it. Presumably, you are going along your daily life and adding and removing tasks from your list. Previously, you learned about moving the tasks around by planning out each day, week, and month but at some point, you will have so many tasks on your list it will be overwhelming. Sometimes because of the complexity of our lives, we just plain have too much to do! We must start asking ourselves hard questions. Should I spend time filling out my daughter's renewal for Girl Scouts even though the troop isn't that active? Should I volunteer at the library book sales or spend my time reading the books I own? Our multifaceted lives require us to make choices and we must realize that we can't possibly do everything we would like to, so this routine is a way to continually re-prioritize.

Also, to help you focus your tasks and remove what is no longer valid, once a year you should set your goals for that year, much like a business sets its annual strategies and budget. Many people use the beginning of the calendar year as that is the time to make New Year's resolutions, a fancy way of setting goals. Since the New Year is so busy with trying to get taxes done, and possibly starting new things in business or other areas, instead try using your birthday as a trigger to set your personal goals for the upcoming year.

✒ Tactic: Setting Routines and Rules for Shared Spaces

If you think of your household like a business, you need a "department" for each of the major parts of running a household. And each department needs a manager who creates the procedures (aka routines) for that department. On the most basic level, someone needs to be responsible for the following departments.

- Housekeeping
- Cleaning
- Financial management
- Reservations/ scheduling
- Kitchen/ meal prep
- Groundskeeping
- Maintenance/ home improvement
- Home administration
- Teacher (if children)

Of all the roles listed, one of the most often overlooked is that of a **home administrator**. However, the home administrator can only be successful if certain elements are put into practice within the common living area.

1. **Create private zones within shared spaces.** Each zone should have clear boundaries and not be places to collect dust. The home administrator should have the authority to enforce that the zones remain intact without too much clutter piling up. This will allow the people cleaning the zone to do their work with minimal additional effort.

   - Each person should have a personal space in the bathroom, kitchen, and common area (such as a living room).
   - Each person should have a transition zone in which to put keys, coats, boots, and items that go in and out regularly.
   - The household should have a convenient place where residents can leave items or messages for each other.

2. **Create household rules.** Throughout this book, I have been listing rules that could help you stay on track and remain organized. Additionally, rules can and should be created for the household. By having written rules, everyone living in the household can be on the same page. They can be as simple as things you would tell a child regarding dinnertime, such as the following:

- No petting the dog at the table.
- Knees under the table when eating.
- Chew with your mouth closed.

Or they can be related to more general life rules such as:

- Ask permission to borrow something that belongs to someone else.
- If you borrow something from someone, give it back when done (or at specified return time, whichever is sooner) and return it in the same condition in which you find it.
- When someone is sleeping or has the door closed, do not disturb him or her.
- Do not interrupt when someone else is speaking.

Keep your running list of rules someplace handy where everyone can reference it. It should be flexible enough to add to it, change it, or delete something from it.

In our household, we had a rule book and it was my youngest son's mission to push each one to the limit without breaking it. One of the rules was, "no playing with water in the house." He proceeded to stand outside the front door and squirt water through the screen.

3. **Create a schedule related to all living in the environment**. At minimum, the schedule should list the following:

- A shared calendar which lists important events such as work schedule. A whiteboard with a section for each person works well for this.
- Schedule for shared responsibilities and chores such as taking out the recycling and paying bills.

📌 Tactic: Discipline

It is not uncommon for me to clear off a space such as a kitchen table with a client only to come back in a week to a cluttered table. If I clear off another space, it will get cluttered very soon after I leave. A good technique would be to clear off the same spot every time and not move on to another area until eventually, it stays clean. Since I am not with the client (aka you), I do not have that luxury so I would suggest looking for patterns. The one pattern that always comes up is the inability to discipline oneself.

To discipline yourself in this endeavor you will need to take the time each day to re-affirm your promise to live a chaos-free life. It also means that you need to muster up the energy now to prepare yourself for your future. If you get off track, get right back on.

A barrier that often rears its ugly self when one is trying to remain disciplined is procrastination, which is your subconscious way of saying you do not want to do something. Below are some common reasons for procrastination and the chapter that each one was addressed.

- I love to do many things. No clear goals. (*SIMPLE*)
- I can't focus (*Slow Down*)
- I don't want to say no (*Get Introspective*)
- I might hurt/anger someone's feelings (*Put Myself First*)
- I have too many trivial tasks in front (*Live in the Present*)
- Everything is too overwhelming (*Lighten your Load*)

If your reason for procrastination is one or more of the above, go back to the corresponding chapter and spend more time committing that concept to memory.

If the entire book has been overwhelming, then discipline yourself to change at least one habit per month or more if necessary. Make sure the new habit has truly sunk in and is easy to maintain before tackling a new one. For example, commit to clear off your desk every day. This one habit will create the most far-reaching changes in your life. You will be able to know what you are doing and you will be able to find the papers needed to do it.

This discipline should not be so strict that you are not having fun. Sometimes, it is good mental health to waste time. You should schedule one day of rest per week. One day where you have no scheduled activities and you decide to do minimal chores.

Finally, the big question is how to discipline yourself in a way as to not let other people keep you from keeping organized for life. For example, it seems that every time I clean out a closet, someone gives me something to fill it up again. Or whenever I get a handle on my workload, my boss gives me more. It is your challenge, as it has been mine, to find your balance and not let others pull you off track.

♀ Taking it Deeper

It may be hard to know what balance feels like because conditions may have brought imbalance at such a young age. As we get older, we don't make time for working through the pain of physical or emotional traumas and we get more unbalanced and eventually sick. We further perpetuate our imbalance and tend to create a setting that is not conducive to healing. There is clutter. Our belongings need attention. People in our lives demand our attention. Or we simply sidetrack ourselves in doing and busying.

People or circumstances may come into our lives to help move us towards balance but we ignore them. One may think it easier to ignore the signs in hopes that the pain will disappear. Well, it won't. It will exacerbate over time unless you treat the underlying pain embedded directly into the body's muscles. And the only way to do that is to give the energy where it is needed. Healing is an everyday endeavor that needs energy.

How does one do it? This brings me right back to time management. How we spend our time on a daily basis will show results. In other words, we reap what we sow. Or for every action, there is an equal and opposite reaction. We can start with shifting our focus ever so slightly and keep up with that one thing for twenty-one days until it becomes a habit. Keeping at it after twenty-one days makes it a routine.

Start with self-care. Make a routine list for yourself. Once you have mastered that, you can move onto a routine for your environmental care. This is where you will start seeing that you have too much in your environment and be able to get organized once and for all. Once you have a handle on taking care of yourself and your environment, you truly start taking care of the world.

📌 Tactic: Live in Harmony with the Environment

Any energy saved in one part of life will naturally be spent in another

If you have gotten this far and are starting to feel more in control, you may want to return to the old ways and say, "I like being fast. Life is too slow now." Let me restate what I stated earlier: It is okay to thrive on chaos but not at the expense of yourself and others. In this section, I will discuss ways to maintain a comfortable life pace and honor the environment and your body rhythms.

Think about what it would have been like to grow up as a pioneer in the 1800's. Life was hard work, but it was also calmer and more nurturing. The pioneers woke up when it was light, worked when something needed to get done, and ate when they were hungry. In the winter, they did more indoor activities. Winter was also a time to rejuvenate and prepare for spring planting, much like a bear or possum hibernates in the winter.

Currently, we do not honor the "slower" pace that winter brings. Also, in the months of summer, more work will not always make the garden grow faster. However, we may not be able to fully go back to honoring the environment because mainstream society today is set up against responding to environmental changes. For example, most people work set hours without regard to the time of year, the rising of the sun, or other factors.

No matter what time of year you are reading this book, you can still practice honoring your body rhythms. Many people try to fight Mother Nature by staying up until 2:00 am and sleeping until noon. When it is dark you should sleep and when it is light you should be awake.

Also, do not fight the seasons. When it is warm, you should spend time outside. When it is cold you should spend time inside rejuvenating. Purchase summer foods in summer. Visit farm stands and enjoy local produce. In this day and age, we have forgotten to listen to our body rhythms and the rhythms of nature.

① Quick Hits

Below are some actions that you can take to continue your pursuit of equilibrium. Some of these have been mentioned in past chapters. Here they are listed in this format so you can transfer them right to your task list.

- **Quit some organized activities to which you belong.** Keep the ones that are most congruent with your purpose and interests. If a hobby becomes a chore, then quit it. You should use the rule of three. No more than three activities. If you have a large family, you may want to limit to one or two activities each. Remember you have to support each other's activities.

- **Practice saying "No."** One of the reasons people complain that they do not have enough time in a day is because they do not say "no" enough. People often take on projects that they think they have to because they feel guilty that they will lose friends, their job, or something else. What they really are losing is autonomy. By saying "yes" without really wanting to do something, a person is taking time from something he wants to do.

- **Analyze your Task List.** Decide if anything can be deleted. Is there busy work that can be eliminated? Are there jobs that belong to or should be done by someone else? What can I delegate? Are there activities that I used to enjoy, but are no longer fun?

- **Eliminate choices.** For example, when grocery shopping always shop at the same store. That way you become familiar with the goods stocked and the way they are arranged. This already eliminates the need to assimilate a new environment. Once you have selected the store at which you will buy groceries, get to know the products that you like. Have you ever walked down the Italian food aisle only to be bombarded with one hundred different varieties of spaghetti sauce from which to choose? Choose one brand or type (put knowledge into choosing it) and stick with it. Write down your choices so you will not forget. Fewer choices mean fewer decisions to take time and energy. This process of eliminating choices does not mean that you cannot try new things. It does mean try it, decide if you will use it again, and stick with your choice.

- **Be open to new things.** Put adventure in your life by budgeting time or money for something new and completely different.

- **Use a budget.** Creating a budget can be a guide for making smart choices. Think about your budget and how much less you will spend on frivolous items.

- **Work when the spirit moves you**. In other words, honor your rhythm of when you are most productive. For example, I am most productive in the morning. So I start working early and get more done before other people even think about being productive. Then when I am least productive in the afternoon, I do busy-work that takes no thinking.

- **Waste time on purpose**. For example, even though you can get to the third-floor office by elevator, take the stairs. It is also healthier to walk the stairs.

- **Allow yourself to be distracted and amazed by things around you.** Look at getting ready in the morning through the eyes of a child. It never ceases to amaze me how many things will distract a four-year-old while brushing her teeth.

- **Plan a day with no appointments or schedule**. In other words, take a vacation at home. On that day, resist every temptation to complete a chore because you have time. Do things that you really enjoy and do something else when you get tired of it. Eat when you are hungry; do not schedule a time.

- **Treat yourself to a day spa, or if you cannot afford it, create your own spa experience.** Start with arising and drinking a large glass of water. Rub yourself down with warm oil. Do yoga or other gentle exercise. Take a bath. Eat slowly. Take an hour to give yourself a pedicure or manicure. Relax in the warmth of the fresh air (or if in winter, sit near the fire and contemplate the flames).

- **Schedule activities that require you to be slower**. For example, hang out in the park and "be."

- **Go on a retreat away from your house, planned around a topic of interest.** Or if you cannot afford it, create your own mini-retreat with close friends or family.

- **Take a vacation or time out in total solitude.** Only bring what you need. Bring two changes of clothes, the ones you are wearing and ones to wear while you are washing the other ones. Make a pact to go nowhere, answer no telephones, and watch no television. Now when you enter back into the everyday world you will remember this solitude time and try to gain a little of it every day. You cannot do that if your time is too full.

- **Ride a bike or walk instead of drive.**

- **Read a book for pleasure.** I always recommend *Atlas Shrugged* by Ayn Rand. It is approximately 1000 pages and makes you think. But in that thinking and self-discovery, my spirit is always raised. I hope yours will be, too.

- **Remember to live in the present.** When you are doing housework, do not give attention to what else you could be doing. "Planning ahead" is different from "living ahead." You cannot eat ahead of time to not have to eat tomorrow.

- **Balance physical activities with mental and spiritual ones.** Do what your body and mind tell you to do. If you have a lot of energy, use it! Do not try to sit down and do paperwork while you are ready to run a marathon. Schedule creative sessions or presentations during your peak time when your cognitive skills are sharpest.

- **Balance the fast times with the slow times**. If you know one time of year will be busy, plan a relaxing time afterward. Do not plan to update your policy manual during the yearly closing of the financial books. If you have a relatively simple life then a complicated vacation might be what you need. If you have a more complicated work-life, then a more simple home life may be in order.

- **Take time for reflection**. This is our body's way of processing what it has been experiencing.

- **Anticipate stress.** Allow extra time when you know you will have a stressful day. Finish a project early to ease the tension of a deadline. Use downtime for thinking to ease the stress that may come later. For example, plan your outfits for the upcoming week so you do not have to think about it while you are stressed. Clean out clutter during summer downtime, instead of during the first week of school or the rush of the holiday season.

- **Pace yourself.** When working on projects, do not try to cram everything in one day. Go back to the planning worksheet and learn to see all the dependent events and start now so you do not have to do it all in a shorter time frame. I often wonder how college students can cram one semester's worth of learning into one all-nighter.

- **Take a break.** No matter how busy you are, always take a breather in the morning and afternoon. This helps change the pace and reminds you what is important in life instead of always living in high gear.

- **Think carefully before taking on new responsibilities.** Let me give an example. Imagine your teenage child wants more responsibility and gets a bank account. However, she cannot manage to balance her checkbook. At some point, she wants to buy a car. How can she handle the responsibility of a car if she can't even keep her checkbook balanced? That said, life is whole, not sequential, and cannot always be put on hold until one skill is perfected before attempting something new. Often moving to the next level forces the old learning to become long-term memory, second nature, and a good habit.

Sometimes you have to create a bypass system, such as in this example, using online banking to compare against your checkbook records and activities.

You are always led back to the path you are supposed to be on.
It is up to you to recognize it and follow it.

Chapter 13 Phase 4- 🕸 Transition

Hopefully, you have read this book slowly and have been able to commit some of the lessons to memory and made the *SIMPLE* Method *a* part of your life. Although I may have opened your eyes to some new concepts that will become part of your life, it will be up to you to make them work for you. Give yourself permission to master the tactics over time. Do not try to retain everything now. Changing habits is an incremental process. Look outside at nature. Good changes take time.

The first step to creating change is **awareness**. By now this is done.

The second step to making a change is **commitment**, which you hopefully did when you signed a covenant with yourself in the *Stabilize* Phase. Continuing with SIMPLE organization is a lifetime commitment. It is not just a nine to five or a once a week thing. For example, I often watch people trying to diet to lose weight. They eat healthy. Eat healthy. Eat healthy. Then all of a sudden, they splurge and have a piece of cake. They think, "I have blown my diet! I may as well have that bag of potato chips and ice cream, too. I can start again tomorrow." It is that thinking which sabotages your efforts. It is consistent with healthy eating which makes people enjoy success in dieting. If you have the piece of cake, then be satisfied with it and stay on track. This is the same concept for everything you commit to in life. And with life organization, 15 minutes a day can go a long way.

Once you have committed, your next step which was mentioned in the *Attain Equilibrium* Chapter is **discipline**. You should check progress every day and give yourself reinforcements. Checking your success every day also helps you evaluate if any adjustments need to be made to your routines. You may want to carry a touchstone to remind yourself of your commitment. Examples of touchstones are a pendant, ring, or something else that you can look at to remind yourself of your success and future success or find a technique that works for you to help you stay on track.

And finally, you will be able to **transition away from this book**. If you decide to leave it on your shelf with the hope of reading it cover to cover at a later date, it will increase frustration and a sense of being stuck. Remember the funnel analogy. Once the opening is clear, things can flow freely in your life.

Although I want you to use this book often as a reference, I don't want you to be in possession of more things than you need. Furthermore, if you have understood the concepts, you will not need to refer to any of these pages because you will have already funneled the concepts into your habits and/or smaller tasks on your Task List. So the final strategy will be to review the information from this book in such a way that you don't need the book any more. The following pages are the place where you can summarize what you have learned with an awareness that once written down, you will prove to yourself and the world that you don't need to rely on a book.

> The only tools you need for survival were given to you at birth - your body and your mind.
>
> Susan Walko

⏱ Quick Hits: **Simplify** Life

My signs that I needed to make a change were:

Sign #1 _____

_____

Sign #2 _____

_____

Sign #3 _____

_____

After completing this book, I realize that I needed to adjust my goals so that they are more attainable and fit with my mission and beliefs.

Mission: _____

_____

Beliefs: _____

_____

Keeping that in mind my goals restated are as follows:

Goal #1 _____

_____

Fits my belief by: _____

_____

Goal #2 _____

_____

Fits my belief by: _____

_____

Goal #3 _____

Fits my belief by: _____

_____

✓ I am remembering the basics of life are a healthy body and a clear mind by taking the following actions:

_____

_____

_____

✓ I have cut out some of the secondary needs I no longer think are necessary.

My top five most important secondary needs are:

_____

_____

_____

_____

_____

Five secondary needs I have decided to cut out are:

_____

_____

_____

_____

_____

⊕ Quick Hits: **S**low Down

✓ I have begun using the funnel system to control inputs coming into my life.

✓ I have stopped trying to fit everything into a day and have begun staging tasks in a way that allows me to slow down.

✓ Other things I have done to slow down are:

_____

_____

_____

_____

① Quick Hits: Get **I**ntrospective

- ✓ I have begun to focus my time and energy on people who help me expand and grow.
- ✓ I have begun to focus my actions so that they are more consistent with my core beliefs.
- ✓ To get introspective, I am personally taking the following steps:

_____

_____

_____

_____

⊕ Quick Hits: Put **M**yself First

✓ Every day I am putting my biggest priorities first.

✓ I regularly set time aside for planning. It is this planning that allows me to be prepared for unexpected events.

✓ Right now my priorities are:

_____

_____

_____

_____

✓ To not put myself by the wayside, I have also started the following:

_____

_____

_____

_____

① Quick Hits: Live in the P̲resent

✓ While I am doing tasks, I am focusing on them because I do not have to remember everything else that I have to do.

✓ Every day I am prioritizing my tasks so I do not have to clutter my mind with details of my undone task list.

✓ You can tell I am living in the present by noticing that I am:

_____

_____

_____

_____

① Quick Hits: Lighten your Load

✓ I have begun making informed choices and eliminating unnecessary choices from my existence.

✓ I have taken actions towards creating zones that are meaningful to my current lifestyle. The zones that are most important to me are:

_____

_____

_____

_____

✓ I have begun eliminating clutter for good and plan to focus on eliminating clutter in the following four areas over the next year:

_____

_____

_____

_____

① Quick Hits: Attain **E**quilibrium

✓ I have established routines for the following sets of tasks:

_____

_____

_____

_____

✓ Other ways that I plan to attain equilibrium for myself.

_____

_____

_____

_____

ⓘ Quick Hits: S.P.O.T.

- ✓ I have successfully moved through the Stabilize Phase because I am no longer feeling that I am spinning out of control.
- ✓ As a result of the Prioritize Phase, daily I am utilizing a task list in which I prioritize and sequence tasks.
- ✓ In the Organize Phase, before physically organizing my stuff and information, I identified zones that are important in my life.
- ✓ Now I am transitioning away from this book.

If I am discussing this book, I would say that the most important thing I learned is:

_____

_____

_____

_____

♀ Taking it Deeper

When I wrote the words for the SIMPLE acronym, I did not realize how appropriate each concept is for many topics. They all have one thing in common and that is someone going through a transition. There are so many little lessons within each concept but each person may learn them differently. Other than life organization, healthy living has been a common theme in my life and thus in this book. See how strategies can apply to the healing journey.

Slow Down. Healing takes time. Make the time. Suspend your usual standards for completing tasks. This also including quieting the mind.

Introspective. Get to know your pain. Feel it. Allow it to surface. When healing, you need to be prepared to go deep. What needs to be healed may seem physical but it is often rooted in emotions that were not expressed.

Myself First. At this time, do not worry about others. It is your journey and to transition you need to take care of yourself. That means listen to your body's cues. Unusual pain could mean something is shifting. Honor it.

Present Living. Don't worry about what you have to get done when your healing process is complete. Don't plan how your life will be different when healing is over. Just be in the present. Feel the emotions that are surfacing. Increase awareness of all that is going on, but don't try to solve everything.

Lighten Your Load. First, start by taking tasks off your list. If they are important enough, they will get done. If not by you, then by someone else. Then let go. Keep shedding.

Equilibrium. When you think you are done healing, you may not be completely done. It most likely took years to get that way and will take a long time to unravel. Trying to break open a flower before it is ready to crack the leaves. The same is true for you, don't try to do it too fast or think you are done healing forever. It may surface again. During healing time, learn your queues so you can notice when it is time to rest and continue healing.

⌂ Life Rules

The next section is a compilation of Organizing and Life Rules mentioned in this book. Please add to it as you uncover rules of your own.

⊕ Quick Hits

- **Take care of yourself.** Every day, eat healthy. Get enough sleep. Exercise- be active and work movement into your day. Rest when needed.

- **Take care of your environment**. Pick up and put away what you use. Clean up after yourself. Care for the items in your possession. Take care of the land.

- **Live humbly.** In other words, don't "need" much and work for what you need.

Thank you for reading this book. If you put the time into it and thought about all of the questions that were posed, then you are hopefully on a path towards life-long organization.

> Many people devote their life to a profession.
>
> Thank God for my profession- living!
>
> Susan Walko, 1986

For printable versions of any of the exercises go to our website at:

http://www.organiz-er.com/publications.html

233

Works Cited

Boll, H. (1963). Anekdote zur Senkund der Arbeitsmoral.

Jess Oppenheimer, M. D. (1952, September 15). *I Love Lucy, Job Switching.* (V. V. Lucille Ball, Performer)

Lindbergh, A. M. (1955). *Gift from the Sea.* New York: Pantheon Books.

Merge, V. (2001). *Who are We?* Kahului: Ringing Cedars Press.

Microsoft. (2020). Clean Up Command. Microsoft.

Index

About the Author

Susan Walko is a born organizer. As a child, Susan organized her toys and games from most played with to least played with. In high school, she color-coded her closet according to activity. By college, Susan was organizing on-campus activities for the student body. As a professional organizer, Susan's firm, Organiz-ER, organizes everything from kitchens to company data files. Now, Susan is offering you her secrets for an organized life that will allow you to spend less time working and taking care of your home, finances, and kids and more time for play.

Susan holds a Bachelor's degree in Accounting and a Master's degree in Personnel. While running a household with four children, a cat, and dog and numerous fish she has managed to simultaneously hold one or two full time jobs. Her lifelong study and passion is the utilization of time.

Made in United States
North Haven, CT
22 October 2021